CONJURIN' OLE TIME

Hoodoo Spells 1800 – 1920

TALIA FELIX

CONJURIN' OLE TIME
Hoodoo Spells 1800 - 1920

Introduction

When it comes to the general public, the style of folk magic that is now called *hoodoo* is a lesser known tradition than its close relative, the religion of Voodoo; and much like Voodoo, it is frequently perceived in the minds of the uninformed to be an inherently evil form of magic or one that focuses solely on curses and harmful spells. Of course, nearly any hoodoo practitioner one is likely to come across has much better things to spend his time at than pointlessly causing curses and deaths; much more often, this kind of magic is used to draw luck, love, money, and other good things from life. Hoodoo is traditionally associated with African-American cultural practices. The ethnographer Friedrich Ratzel, writing in the 19th century about this traditionally African-American practice, declared: "Witchcraft indeed is really the one thing that makes the negro's life worth living. What wonder if he attaches a great value to it?"

Yet while hoodoo is ostensibly derived from African magical practices that were brought to American soils by the slave trade, hoodoo nevertheless did not become *hoodoo* until that point when it hit the states. It's no more fair to call such a practice "African" than it is to apply such an adjective to jazz or rock music, which certainly have their African ancestors; but no one would take West African djembe drumming for jazz, without the help of some western instruments, and neither would traditional Appalachian folk music ever be taken for rock without the help of African influences.

Some have tried to compensate for this complicated situation by labeling hoodoo as "African-American magic" but, as one black girl I used to know complained in frustration about the very label of African-American, "No one in my family has been from Africa for two hundred years!" Even rather early accounts of hoodoo and Voodoo practices mention whites as well as blacks participating in the rites, suggesting it's always been something of a mixed bag.

In early American sources one sometimes finds the accounts of "negro witchcraft" to label the practice as obeah, an African word which ceased to be used in reference to United States magical practice by the middle 19th century. In its place sprouts *voodoo* (1850), *hoodoo* (1870), *goopher* (1887), and *conjuration* (an old word originally used for any type of magic.)

A certain author who flourished around the turn of the 20th century, named Charles W. Chesnutt (who interestingly had some mixed blood of his own; he considered himself to be black though admitting he was 7/8ths white) wrote the following on the topic of "conjuration" and "goopher":

"It probably grew, in the first place, out of African fetichism ... Certain features, too, suggest a distant affinity with Voodooism, or snake worship, a cult which seems to have been indigenous to tropical America. These beliefs, which in the place of their origin had all the sanctions of religion and social custom, became, in the shadow of the white man's civilization, a pale reflection of their former selves. In time, too, they were mingled and confused with the witchcraft and ghost lore of the white man, and the tricks and delusions of the Indian conjurer."

So he wrote in the year 1901, scarcely more than forty years after the final slave ship had come to the United States.

* * *

A few years ago I produced a little booklet by the title of *The Conjure Cookbook*, which was an effort to compile a hoodoo style formulary of magical potions. When researching the *Cookbook*,

I often came upon what one would presently consider to be charms and spells of hoodoo, yet from some surprisingly old sources. One Johann Jacob Wecker, who lived from 1528 to 1586, advised about the conjure curio of the swallow's heart which remains popular today with the hoodoo crowd. Wecker promised that "All men will love thee, if thou carry with thee a Swallows heart." Elsewhere in the same book he recommends using lodestones for similar purpose and indicates Albertus Magnus to have been his source. Wecker even talks a little about African magic.

In the 19th and 20th centuries, publishing houses like M. Young and De Laurence Scott and Co. would spit out cheap occult books cobbled together from various public domain sources (a practice which is still done today) with the effect that new generations were exposed to magical material dating all the way back to the Renaissance. Some of these publishers even targeted an African-American customer base, thereby saturating old African magical customs with the habits of European grimoire spells. In other instances, old spells that had been around for ages and had entered the folk magic of Europe and America alike were taken up by the hoodoo men. One such example: Charles Godfrey Leland, in his book *Gypsy Sorcery and Fortune Telling* (1891) repeats as a gypsy spell, learned in his research in Europe, the talismanic charm of wearing a bat's heart bound to the arm with red thread or ribbon to win at gambling; this same spell is given in *Pow-Wow's; or, The Long Lost Friend* (1820) which scarcely even presents its advice as magic but rather as everyday advice for American farmers. In the early 20th century, when Harry M. Hyatt went to collect oral accounts of hoodoo spells, several of his black informants recited the same trick.

In addition to all this, there is probably even more American Indian lore worked into hoodoo than the written records make apparent. Coincidental similarities in practice made some borrowing easy between the Native and the new cultures – for example, the likeness between the Indian medicine bag and the African mojo. It is also assumed that it was the Indians who taught the whites and blacks the properties of the new world herbs and plants. Some species like "American Mandrake" are obviously named to mark them as replacements for European herbs possessed with similar assets.

When the idea came to me of collecting a book of old time hoodoo, the first problem became that of *how old-time is old time hoodoo?* In *Conjure Cookbook* I found myself typing up recipes that went all the way back to the time of Moses. Is that hoodoo or not? (Hurston certainly claims he was the first hoodoo man.) For the purpose of the Cookbook I had decided that the age of the recipes wouldn't matter, but for a book with a particular focus on the age of the recipes it would certainly be an important distinction. How old is old – and how old is hoodoo?

I finally decided on the following criteria:

◆ 1800 would be used as an approximate start date. Though hoodoo-esque magic in America is known before then (the oldest I've heard being the magical rye cake of Tituba the slave which set off that famous matter in Salem, Massachusetts [+])

[+] Tituba's magical concoction consisted of a rye cake, "which she salted in a peculiar manner," and which was baked inside cabbage leaves in the embers of a fire. The plan was that the Parris children, who were believed to be suffering from the ill effects of witchcraft, would see a vision or other cue as to whom had bewitched them upon eating these cakes. Unfortunately for poor Tituba, the children identified her as the culprit – even though they had refused to actually eat the cakes.

It is of note that in Christian European cultures, while witchcraft and magic spells were usually frowned upon (at the very least), spells it's exceedingly rare to find any detailed accounts of hoodoo or conjure tricks before the middle of the 19th century; consequently, to call the book *Conjure Spells 1650-1920* when I might be lucky to find one complete spell dating anything before 1790 would just be too misleading. Magic had gone somewhat out of fashion during the Age of Enlightenment, and it wasn't until the 19th century that interest in folklore and superstition emerged again amongst literate people, making research materials much easier to come by from that time onward. It therefore seemed like a good place to start.

◆The source had to be, in some kind of manner, American – either written, spoken or published by Americans, popular in America, or else written reliably about Americans be they black or otherwise. This means reprints of European and other magic spells can count as hoodoo as long as there's probability that some American magician would have been able to read them and learn from them. Of course I am using some discretion on this and not just including any old magical text that was put to print during the timeframe;

---

to prevent one from becoming the victim of evil witchcraft were often felt to be an exception to this rule, hence the Parris family's willingness to let Tituba do her work described above. Additionally, it is useful to remember that the lines between magic and science used to be much more blurry, and from ancient times right through the 19th century many things which we nowadays would view as magic or witchcraft would have been seen as science or medicine. Wecker and Culpeper are excellent examples of this.

when possible I have tried to use texts that I know were marketed to magical practitioners (such as titles printed by the De Laurence company) or else texts where the magical methods described ring familiar (as with some of Leland's "Etruscan Magic" which involves little red bags filled with herbs, much in the style of the hoodoo mojo bag. Leland himself was American and made frequent references to Voodoo practice in that same book.)

The sourcebooks fall into three categories: books that were definitely used by hoodoo practitioners (such as the *6th and 7th Books of Moses*, which were often referenced), books that were probably used by practitioners (such as the *Grimoire of St. Cyprian*, which includes unusual spells that seem to have been preserved in the practice even if I've never come across a direct mention of the book by a hoodoo worker of old) and books that would have been available to practitioners even if there's no proof one way or another for their use. In this last case I'm using my judgment and trying to include only magical texts of the era that seem to link or mimic other known hoodoo rites which I have encountered during my research. It's of note that some texts of this type may date to earlier than 1800.

◆ 1920 would be used as the cutoff date for "old time." This is around the era where the curio catalogues and occult supply houses began to spring up and saturate the markets with prepared formulas, thereby changing the style of practice to the more modern "urban" mode which is generally encountered today. In fact, I had originally intended to use a later cutoff date, 1930, for this work; yet when I began to collect my notes, I found the style of hoodoo magic to change so clearly and abruptly post-1920 that the practice had nearly become a new style of magic altogether. The 1920s were definitely the end of the Old Time practice. Nevertheless, certain works that were published after 1920 but which describe events and practices from before that time would still be eligible for use, such as the famous *Hoodoo - Rootwork - Conjuration - Witchcraft* collection of Harry M. Hyatt.

As this is meant to be a something of a practical guide rather than merely a scholarly or historical study, I have generally left out all but the most unusual of the old time health remedies, even though it seems that herbal medicine was actually a large portion of what was considered to be hoodoo, and it appears that such medical practice would have been a major part of almost any conjure doctor's business. Though charms to protect against common ailments like "rheumatism" (which is no longer even considered to be a disease) and to help babies teeth are amongst the most easily found and best recorded of formulas, I have felt that modern medicine can and should be used to much better effect in most of these cases, and that such spells would therefore be of little use to the reader who turns to this text for the sake of learning the practice of authentic, traditional magic. I myself am guilty of having initially learned my hoodoo from curio catalogues and botanica chapbooks: it is my own obsessive nature that drew me further and further back through the written records, trying to find out more about this fascinating practice. Here's hoping to present a collection of authentic old time spells which, even if people choose not to use them, might at least help preserve knowledge of their working in one easy to use collection. It is unfortunate that this endeavor is bound to be somewhat incomplete, for I am restricted to writing only on what spells and practices managed to make their way into print during a time when hoodoo was not usually viewed as a pursuit of the literate and educated.

Still, I know it took me a lot longer than expected to assemble all this data; but I've gone and done it so that you don't have to.

Items &
Elements of
Conjure

HIGH JOHN THE CONQUEROR ROOT

Conqueror roots have been used to bestow great powers upon the bearer. It was reported in the 19th century that "All believers in conjuring quake when they see a bit of it in the hand of any one." Old sources also call this root Conquer-John or High John. A. C. Holbert in 1905 wrote that it was "always an ingredient in [negro] 'charm bags' and their voodoo rites and philtres." Modern hoodoo generally expects the Conqueror root to be the root of *ipomoea jalapa,* also called jalap root.

However, as far as history goes, it appears that things were not always so consistent. Many of the old time practitioners gathered their own herbs and roots from the wilderness, and what grows in Florida might not grow in Illinois. 19th century sources can identify the Conqueror root to come from quite a variety of different plants, and several of the old time uses for John roots and plants don't make sense if one tries to do them with a jalap root: for example, the red seeds of the plant were said to be used for harmful magic, and bark from the plant was used to make a wrapping for other charms; yet the seeds of the jalap are not red, and the plant is a kind of morning glory vine which doesn't possess much in the way of bark. There is also the little matter of fact that jalap root isn't actually even native to the United States and so could have never been wild-gathered by the traditional practitioners.

If not jalap, what, then, is the genuine John

the Conqueror root? Old time candidates for the High John the Conqueror plant include Jack-in-the-pulpit, Solomon's seal (great or dwarf), other kinds of morning glories (the kind called big-root morning glory being especially popular), tormentil, colicroot, wood geranium, and Sampson snake root. Several modern sourcebooks exist that say Conqueror root comes from the St. John's wort plant, but this seems unlikely as the roots of this plant are very small and fine; additionally, their use never turns up in any magic prior to the appearance of this claim in the later 20th century. Solomon's seal root seems to be the one root identified most commonly in the historical sources as being the John the Conqueror root. I have yet to find a text before 1920 that identifies it as jalap.

It is speculated by many that High John the Conqueror evolved as a New World replacement for other roots used in African magic, such as the Kongo munkwiza root which was held by chiefs as a symbol of power and even reputed to be what bestowed it. This could account for the variety of herbs and roots which have passed as High John; if more than one replacement was attempted throughout various places or by various folks, of course there would be several different plants employed.

THE RABBIT'S FOOT

"De luckiest luck is rabbit foot luck."

Most Americans are familiar with the concept of the lucky rabbit's foot, but few know the formal process required for creating one. Here is the description according to the *Journal of American Folklore*.

"*The rabbit's foot is esteemed a powerful talisman to bring good fortune to the wearer and protect him from all danger. As this belief is more or less common throughout the South, it may be well to state how the charm is prepared, for the benefit of those who wish to be put on the royal road to health, wealth, and prosperity. It must be the left hind foot of a graveyard rabbit, i. e., one caught in a graveyard, although one captured under the gallows would probably answer as well. It must be taken at the midnight hour, the foot amputated, and the rabbit released, if not killed in the capture. The foot must then be carried secretly in the pocket until by chance the owner happens upon a hollow stump in which water has collected from recent rains. The foot is then dipped (three times?) into this water and the charm is complete. Among the negroes and the uneducated whites of the South the reputed possessor of this potent talisman is at once feared and respected. The phenomenal success of General Fitzhugh Lee of Virginia in his gubernatorial race was attributed by the negroes to the fact that he carried a rabbit's foot and a bottle of stump water. A rabbit's foot was also sent to President Cleveland, together with other fetiches, by a Texas admirer, at the outset of his administration.*"

Another source adds that the capturing of the rabbit should be done on a cloudy night of a new moon, and another also suggests that the aforementioned conditions should all be met on a Friday the 13th for best potency. It was apparently also considered equally auspicious if the rabbit were simply captured by a seventh son of a seventh son or other supernaturally gifted person. (Seventh sons of sevenths sons have long been attributed with possessing special luck or power, in European folklore.) Sometimes one foot or the other was believed to carry the superior luck, but there doesn't seem to be consistency as to which – although analyzing the data leads one to suspect whites seem to favor the left while blacks apparently favor the right.

Carrying a rabbit or hare's foot is an old tradition of European origin. The Englishman Samuel Pepys, in 1664, bore one to help with his gastro-intestinal problems, but discovered after a few weeks that the foot he carried was incorrectly made ("my hare's foote hath not the joynt to it.") After correcting the problem he reported a great and immediate improvement to his health. Many historical sources indicate properties of health and wellness as the primary use for rabbit's feet – one early 20th century dentist even claimed to use them on his patients instead of anaesthesia!

In hoodoo practice, rabbit's feet were employed by wearing them on the body or the clothing, carrying them inside a charm or mojo hand, or by touching the foot to the body part affected. European tradition also saw them hung over doorways. By the later 19th century, the rabbit's foot was frequently mentioned amongst the materials used by negro magical practitioners. A person writing only under the alias "Unicorn" tells about a famous Tennessee rabbit hunter he'd known in his youth called Nat Langan, to whom he attributes the explanation for its popularity: "Colored people ... think a rabbit has got the sense to outwit any other animal, or all of 'em put together." It's said that the hare is a popular figure in traditional African folktales as well as Creek and Cherokee Indian oral legends, in which he's considered a trickster figure.

Lucky mole paws (cut from the live animal) or lucky turkey's feet are also known charms with similar properties. For those who cannot come across a proper rabbit's foot or who are unwilling to harm animals, the buckeye nut, by tradition, is also alleged to hold many of the same properties.

THE DEAD

Ancestor worship, also called — perhaps more accurately — *ancestor veneration*, exists in many cultures and is a prevalent practice amongst many African tribes. The term ancestor "worship" should not be taken to mean that the dead are considered to be gods or god-like, but rather that they are believed to still have the power to affect and influence the world of the living and are therefore presumed to still require care and sustenance.

Ancestors are presumed to have the most vested interest in preserving social orders on earth, and they offer a link between the divine world and the mundane which entitles them to a special place as the go-to source for any spiritual help needed by their descendants.

And yet, in old time hoodoo practice, the documented reports suggest that it is not beloved ancestor's graves that are most highly sought by the American hoodoo man for aiding in his magical intents, but the graves of those poor souls who "died bad" (that is, unnatural death — especially by murder or suicide) or else people whose situation in life related in some way to the circumstances one desires to bring about, such as a gambler's grave to improve one's luck with money. This would appear to bear a more like resemblance to a practice of African magic called *muti*, where people of certain conditions are specifically murdered or sacrificed in order to use their bodies for spells. It is a practice still followed today: "The victim is not first killed and the parts removed," a recent article reports, "No, for if the medicine is to have greatest effect the parts in question, limbs, genitals, eyes, ears, even the whole skin, must be removed while he or she is still alive, in the belief that their agonising screams add to the potency of the magic." Several hoodoo beliefs using parts of animals echo this particular notion, such as the black cat bone spell wherein a cat is boiled alive to provide a lucky bone, or the belief that a mole's paw cut only from the live animal could bring luck. The 21st century African film director Neill Blomkamp, in his commentary on his own movie *District 9,* describes a practice in modern African muti of using dead men's hands to attract good luck — he even remarks on its similarities to American Voodoo. Compare to the report of American author James William Buel around the year 1880: "In earlier years grave-yards were frequently desecrated by negro resurrectionists whose sole impulse was to obtain parts of the corpse from which to make charms. It is even now common for negroes to carry about on their persons the hand of a dead man or woman, with all the putrifying flesh attached. Bodies of murdered men are most sought for, as these are regarded as possessing greater mystic virtue than the bones of one that has come to a natural death. It may be asserted [many negroes] ... carry either in their pockets or attached to strings about their necks, finger-bones of a human hand. The thumb is more generally used as an amulet, but every finger-bone is regarded as being very efficacious in bringing good luck."

Retrieving body parts from strangers' graves certainly does not appear to have been a common custom of ancestor worship. Does American hoodoo derive the preference for those who "died bad" as a replacement for the ritual medicine murders of Africa?

The popular conjure ingredient of grave dirt appears to be another item of Atlantic African origin: in historical sources it is typically mentioned as being used in hoodoo or obeah rites, but rarely ever in European spells. The grave dirt's power is provided by the spirit of the person from whose grave it is taken: it can be added to mojo charms, powder blends, or sprinkled alone to produce its desired effect, which can range from working love spells to deadly curses. Typically, it is expected that a few coins, or some food or drink will be left on the grave as payment for the service of the one from whose grave the dirt has been taken. Some of the old accounts specify the dirt should be taken from particular spots on the grave (as at the foot of the grave, in the center of the grave by the heart, from the dirt that touches the coffin, etc.) or that it should be collected at certain times (such as the dark of the moon, or at midnight.) It was apparently felt that the grave dirt would only possess an effect for the person it was intended to be used against, and it could otherwise be handled freely by the magical practitioners or by innocent bystanders. Buel provides further information, writing of the hoodoo belief that "every instrument causing death is endowed with a supernatural power which may be utilized by any one who possesses the ghostly trophy ... We have now the horrifying spectacle of a greedy scramble among white men and women every time an official execution takes place, to obtain pieces of the rope with which the hanging was accomplished, and sometimes parts of the scaffold are also broken off and preserved by superstitious persons." Buel assumed the belief in the beneficial powers of the dead to be of purely African origin, but employing the dead or their associated artifacts for drawing positive influences is also traditional amongst whites. European grimoire spells make use of funeral shrouds, graves, and ropes from hanged men in gambling and money drawing rites. Love potions could include the flesh of a thief amongst the ingredient list. In England, a law was passed in 1604 forbidding anyone to "take any dead man woman or child out of his her or theire grave ... or the skin, bone or any other parte of any dead person, to be imployed or used in any manner of Witchecrafte, Sorcerie, Charme or Inchantment," suggesting that people had been so doing up till that time. A powder called *mummia*, originally made from pulverizing Egyptian mummies and later made from any kind of dried human remains, was a popular medicine in Europe in the middle ages and remained available for purchase from legitimate medical suppliers as late as 1908: it was believed to be efficacious for preventing decay and degeneration of the body if swallowed or applied, and was even added to artists paint in the belief it would prevent colors from fading. Even the very concept of the holy relic – preserved body parts from saints, still believed to possess special abilities to bless those who would come into their presence – proves the European's view of the dead was not purely negative. Use of coffin hardware, often as a protective or medicinal agent, is known from European magic: rings from a coffin were used against colic and digestive troubles; coffin nails were used against epilepsy, rheumatism, toothache and other ailments; funeral shrouds were employed as a power-enhancer. But the dead of Europe did have their harmful use, too: a German spell to cause death was to put a coffin nail into a living victim's shoe, and a Danish/German spell to bring about someone's death was to put a piece of the victim's clothing onto a corpse so he would sicken and die as the garment rotted with the dead man.

Old reports claiming to detail Voodoo in America sometimes make reference to cannibalism as being a part of the practice. An article in the *Journal of American Folklore* describes a case circa 1885 wherein "an old negress ... had cut up a small child and salted it away in a barrel," but notes that there was no evidence for the crime being related to any occult practice. I, too, have found no knowledgeable accounts of old style hoodoo or Voodoo that I would classify to include cannibalism (though by a stretch one could claim certain love spells, whereby one feeds their own hair, skin or blood to a potential lover, might be able to count.) However, given the frequency of the claim, and the fact that cannibalism is still known to occur in certain instances in modern Africa — with recent examples in Liberia, Congo and Sierra Leone — it seems possible that some early slaves may have initially attempted to preserve this practice, and the stories it bred kept circulating for a few generations even after it was discontinued. At the same time, the European beliefs and claims that witches would eat babies were also popular from the middle ages onward, and yet have little worthy evidence for support; so it may just be one of those things people always *say* about witchcraft, but nothing more.

BLACK CAT BONE

"The Trick Bone Of A Black Cat. — Put ashes and water into a pot, set it over a fire and let it come to a boil. Have ready a black cat (not a strand of white hair on him), cut his head off, put him in the lye, and let boil until all the flesh has left the bones. Take out every bone. Wash them. Now for finding the luck bone; take up one bone, place it in your mouth, and ask your partner, 'Do you see me?' If he says yes, you will have to try another, asking the same question every time. When you. put the witchy bone in your mouth he will say, 'I don't see you.' Then take that bone, put it in your pocket and keep it there, and you can steal anything you want and no one will see. In fact, you can do any kind of trick you want, and no one will know it.

"Another informant tells us that the lucky bone will rise to the top when the flesh has all boiled off from the bones." Note. — It is sufficiently remarkable, and full of instruction in regard to the origins of American negro folk-lore, that this superstition also

belongs to Germans in Canada, and is plainly of European descent."

Harry M. Hyatt recorded a great many variations on the black cat ritual, of which but one version is given above; sometimes the feline's special bone was said to be identifiable by taste; some versions specified dumping the bones in a river or letting the bones sit out under a tree in order to select the magic bone, which would behave in some peculiar way; others merely described where in the body the bone would be found (usually it was said to be a "wishbone" or else a bone from the cat's chest or from its back.) Most versions indicate the cat should be boiled while still alive; however, there were a few variations that specified, to the contrary, that the cat should first be killed more humanely

so that its power wouldn't be "weakened" by pain or fright. One informant even suggested omitting the boiling and just letting the carcass of a murdered cat skeletonize in a box. Once the specially empowered cat bone was acquired, it would be used by holding it in the mouth, wearing it on a string or placing it in a bag. Sometime it was said that the bone needed additional dressings to ensure it would be effective.

Possibly the oldest version of the spell comes from the *Book of St. Cyprian,* many grimoires were falsely attributed to this saint, who according to legend had been a great magician before his conversion to Christianity. Currently, it is generally agreed that his actual authorship of the book in question would be unlikely, as no records of such a text exist before the 19th century; but with the first known versions appearing in the 1800s it still predates any other records of the Black Cat rite that I know of. The book appears to have been originally written in Portuguese and became influential first in South American magical practices such as Candomble. Cyprian's version of the black cat spell says to boil the cat with willow wood and *sementes brancas* (literally "white seeds" or "white grains") until the meat falls from the bones. The bones should be strained and one by one placed in the practitioner's mouth as he sits before a mirror. When the magical bone is placed in the mouth, he will become invisible (or, as one of Hyatt's informants described it, the mirror would fog up or become blurry.) Interestingly, many of Hyatt's informants said particularly that the black cat should not have "a single white hair." The Cyprian grimoire does not say this about the boiled cat spell, but another black cat rite in the same book wherein a cat is tied up and offered to the devil, does include this direction. It is also notable that one Hyatt informant recommended just using any color of cat and simply painting it black before beginning.

The traditional use of the cat bone is to turn the user invisible, but over time its reputation grew to include the ability to provide the user with mastery of other kinds of supernatural powers, or the ability to bring good gambling luck, or to escape the law, or to bestow the magical force to control others or command love. Aches and pains rubbed with the bone would be cured instantly. It was so powerful that merely tracing such a magic bone and keeping the tracing could be almost as powerful as the bone itself. I have concluded — and have had confirmed to me by a living practitioner — that the original and most genuine "Black Cat Oils" were made from the grease left behind in the kettle by the cat's boiling process.

Additionally I did find one old black cat rite where it was specified that, after all was said and done, one could save the pot liquid and reuse it as a floor wash by mixing it with cinnamon and bergamot oils, and some sugar, to attract money.

SNAKES

Snakes have traditionally held such an important status in Voodoo ceremonies that the practice is often referred to, in older sources, as "snake worship." Jeffrey E. Anderson writes that the African snake god, Da, chief of the earth deities in Dahomey culture, "merged with that of Indian deities. Snake gods and spirits were plentiful in the beliefs of southeastern Indians. [...] Indians set snakes apart from other animals because of their lack of appendages, crediting them with power over other animals, plants, and the elements." Further conflation of the legends with the Christian concept of the snake as the Devil — a trickster and evildoer — can be found; one folklore account which attempted to explain the snake's importance in hoodoo, was given in which it was said that after successfully tempting Adam and Eve, the Old Testament serpent laughed so hard that he split in two. The spirit part of him "go roun' now, temptin' folks ter sin, an' he'pin' de Hoodoos." The other part, his body, became the snakes which live in graveyards, where they now stay and mourn over the mortality and death they have brought into the world. These cemetery snakes were said to be especially powerful creatures when employed for magical use, particularly for wicked intentions as it was supposed to be the Devil himself providing this aid.

Snakes and their body parts are mainly used in hoodoo practices for the purpose of doing harm and evil, with protective powers being a secondary use. Occasionally they are employed in spells meant to bring wisdom or magical powers to the practitioner. For all magical uses, rattlesnakes are considered to be especially powerful and above all the other species of serpents.

CONJURE BAGS, HANDS, MOJOS and GRIS-GRIS

Mojo bags and gris-gris bags are generally small cloth pouches or bundles containing curios, which create various influences upon the people for whom they are constructed. Descriptions of old time conjure bags usually portray them as being filled with herbs, roots, powders, animal or human parts, metallic objects like nails or coins, animal or human hair, bits of cloth, and ashes. It is notable that many hoodoo spellcasters of the past seem to have enjoyed a practice of scorching herbs and other materials in a pan before putting them to use: the frequent inclusion of apparent "ashes" in these charms may be a result of this particular work-method. The conjure bag's origins seem to come mainly from a conflation of two African customs: The Mojo and the Gris-Gris.

It is of note that I cannot find a source for the actual word "mojo" before 1920, and I only even use the word here because it has come to be the usual designation for these items throughout most of the US. Dictionaries give a general date of the late 1920s for the term's first appearance in English, and claim it is from Gullah *moco*, meaning "witchcraft," and ultimately from the Fulani language. Other sources claim it is a word of Kongo origin, derived apparently from the word *mooyo*, a word that can mean "life" and which Jeffrey A. Anderson says "referred to spirits that dwelt within magical charms and was easily transferred to the spirits' dwelling place." According to Kongo belief, entities called *minkisi* reside inside of all magical charms and provide them their power; the mooyo essence is combined with additional ingredients in order to direct the spirit as needed. The term minkisi (singular: nkisi) is most often applied to humanoid statues that might have more in common with the classic image of the "voodoo doll" than with the mojo as we know it, but other items too can serve as their receptacles including shells, pots and packets.

The gris-gris or "Gregory bag" also originated as an African charm and the word itself is of Mande origin. It is sometimes rumored that the word means "grey-grey" due to the French word for grey being *gris*, but the sound-alike is coincidental. The original gris-gris were seemingly made primarily out of verses from the Koran, chosen for specific purposes and carried on the person. The Koran is believed by tradition to be the literal word of God, and so for a Muslim its verses would make a potent charm indeed. Once the rite was Americanized and thereby Christianized,

Bible verses sometimes took the place of the old Koran segments. Sigils, presumably of African origin, are also mentioned to have been used in the bags from at least the year 1800. This then aligned itself with some European grimoire trad-ition, and magical seals and talismans from works like *The 6th and 7th Books of Moses* and *The Black Pullet* came to be included in the gris-gris once literacy made them accessible.

The traditional gris-gris of modern Africa are most commonly wrapped in leather, though other casings may be used depending upon the purpose of the charm. Nicholas Owen, an 18th century slave trader, also confirmed leather as the primary wrapping of his day. Later descriptions, from the late 19th century onward, tell of bags made from multiple colors of material layered together: usually cloth or leather. Gris-gris are still made this way around New Orleans, and strong, contrasting colors are a frequent and important aesthetic element in many African-American crafts. Mojos could be made in other ways as well: Red flannel was considered to be a powerful ingredient in spells all on its own, and many mojos and gris-gris either included the material in the contents or wrappings, or were fashioned in whole bags made from red flannel. Leather was also a common outer-wrapping, linking back to the African gris-gris and the American Indian medicine bag. Ill-intentioned mojos were said to find their power enhanced if they used skin cut from a still-living cat in the wrappings. Some gris-gris also were encased in metal; this could be done both instead of and in addition to the cloth or leather wrappings. It was said that mojo charms were instructed to never be tied with knots, as such would interfere with the indwelling spirit's free movement, but a string could be wrapped around them for security's sake.

The mojo seems to have also aligned itself either by coincidental similarity or by intentional conflation with the American Indian "medicine bag," which also uses a pouch filled with a variety of items to work supernatural influences. Period sources are often not very good at differentiating one tribe's tradition from another, so it can be hard to discern what is "standard" or if there even is such designation. Minerals alone are often described as filling the medicine bags in-period. Modern sources claim that a traditional Indian medicine bag contains at least one item each from the categories of mineral, animal, plant and man-made, and that hair and nail clippings from the shaman who created the bag can be included, too — a trait that makes sense of some old conjure bag descriptions, wherein hair from apparently unknown persons are included. An influential 19th century account by George Caitlin tells that medicine bags were "constructed of the skins of animals, of birds, or of reptiles, and ornamented and preserved in a thousand different ways ... These skins are generally attached to some part of the clothing of the Indian, or carried in his hand. They are oftentimes decorated in such a manner as to be exceedingly ornamental to his person, and always are stuffed with grass, or moss, or something of the kind; and generally without drugs or medicines within them, as they are religiously closed and sealed, and are seldom, if ever, opened. I find that every Indian in his primitive state carries his medicine-bag in some form or other, to which he pays the greatest homage ... it would seem in some instances as if he actually worshipped it. Feasts are often made, and dogs and horses sacrificed, to a man's medicine and days, and even weeks, of fasting and penance of various kinds are often suffered to appease his medicine, which he imagines he has in some way offended.

"... The manner in which this curious and important article is instituted is this: a boy, at the age of fourteen or fifteen years ... [l]ies down[] on the ground in some remote or secluded spot, crying to the Great Spirit, and fasting the whole time. ... when he falls asleep, the first animal, bird, or reptile, of which he dreams (or pretends to have dreamed, perhaps), he considers the Great Spirit has designated for his mysterious protector through life. He then returns home to his father's lodge, and relates his success; and after allaying his thirst, and satiating his appetite, he sallies forth with weapons or traps, until he can procure the animal or bird, the skin of which he preserves entire, and ornaments it according to his own fancy, and carries it with him through life, for 'good luck' (as he calls it); as his strength in battle, and in death his guardian Spirit, that is buried with him; and which is to conduct him safe to the beautiful hunting grounds, which he contemplates in the world to come.

"The value of the medicine-bag to the Indian is beyond all price; ... An Indian carries his medicine-bag into battle, and trusts to it for his protection; and if he loses it ... the loser is cut short of the respect that is due to other young men of his tribe, and for ever subject to the degrading epithet of 'a man without medicine,' or 'he who has lost his medicine,' until he can replace it again, which can only be done by rushing into battle and plundering one from an enemy whom he slays with his own hand."

Another account mentions that the Indians considered it very unlucky to allow any other person to touch or examine one's medicine bag. This belief seems to persist regarding the mojo — in modern lore it is said that such a charm will lose its power if someone other than the user lays hands on the finished item.

The conjure bag of old is usually described to have been a little smaller than the modern variants one typically sees. They were presented by various sources as being about the size of a walnut, or smaller; though by 1920 their proportions were starting to increase — an account of Kentucky superstition published in that year gives a bag's dimensions as being "about six by four inches in size." Traditionally the finished charms were fed with whiskey, which during the designated timeframe would usually mean rye whiskey or "moonshine" corn whiskey. It appears that the libation was commonly poured first into the user's mouth and then spat onto the bag, sometimes accompanied with spoken words. An ex-slave named Henry F. Pyles told the story of a love-drawing hand he was given and how he was supposed to spit whiskey over it before putting it to use; unfortunately in the excitement he kept swallowing and choking on the liquor or spitting but missing the bag altogether (another testament to the small size of these charms.) An alternate way to feed the bags was to soak them in the needed substance. By the end of the 19th century alcohol-based perfumes were becoming a more common feed for the conjure bags. Oils or greases, infused with magical herbs, were also used as a feed for the devices, though this seems to have been employed much less commonly than the alcoholic substances. A 19th century hoodoo man and former slave called King Alexander, claimed that alcohol was the usual food for similar charms in Africa; oil-feedings may have then evolved from a different tradition, such as the Judeo-Christian practice of blessing and consecrating objects with anointing oils.

BOTTLES and GOURDS

Old time hoodoo bottle spells seem to be nearly always of a harmful or negative nature; or at least this is the case with the ones that made it into whatever historical records I could access. Jeffrey E. Anderson writes in his book *Conjure in African American Society,* "An evil charm that originated in Europe was the conjure bottle. Conjure bottles were glass containers filled with harmful magical items. They took the place of malevolent conjure bags in some areas, particularly those settled by the English." English bottle spells, called "Witch Bottles" were traditionally of a protective nature, but they did generally include unpleasant items like pins, nails and urine. Examples of them have been found in America, always in glass bottles, and commonly buried or placed upside down. The

U.S. examples usually contained pins or nails like the European bottles, plus other ingredients which are traditionally employed for harmful conjure; for obvious reasons they were also more likely to contain liquid ingredients than the otherwise similar cloth and leather mojo bags. The sole historical account I've seen of a protective US conjure bottle which specifically stated this to be its purpose, came from an incident dated 1877, of a white family near Savannah, Georgia who kept "a black bottle containing iron nails ... under the front door-step" in order ""to keep witches off the place.""

The gourd is a related magical tool to the bottle. African gourd charms are said to be known for both good and evil (though the negative intention is, again, better documented) and are sometimes considered to be the predecessor of hoodoo style bottle spells: Mary Alicia Owen's informant, King Alexander, reported using one while he was a slave; it was intended to drive away a rival conjure doctor. His gourd was filled with the victim's personal items plus red clover leaves, alum, snakeroot, and mayapple leaves, and sailed down the river along with a command that "he whose life is in you follow you." One of the oldest hoodoo spells I've ever found was a gourd spell, used in 1793: "a callibash full of feathers and claws of birds, mixed with negro men's nails" was given by an African-born slave to some young friends of his, with the intent that it "soften the severity of their master." The master soon afterwards became ill, and the gourd was blamed as the cause.

SIGILS and SACRED WRITINGS

"Historically what denoted a sigil was extremely varied. The only true criteria was that it be an image and have magical properties." So says the Akashic Records website, summarizing it just as well as I could. The use of magical symbols has been known throughout the world, and sensibly it has entered hoodoo practice too. Books like the *Black Pullet*, the *Petit Albert* and *The Great Book of Magical Art and Hindu Magic* (which despite its name has nothing to do with Hinduism) are full of European magical sigils that have become popular amongst hoodoo practitioners. The much beloved *Sixth and Seventh Books of Moses* is practically nothing but a collection of sigils, in the form of seals and "tables of spirits" which one uses according to specified methods, to achieve purposes ranging from control of spirits to good luck in gambling.

Perhaps the most common magical image found in hoodoo is the x or + shape of two lines intersecting. It is said to be derived from the Kongo Cosmogram, a more elaborate design of a + shape surrounded with arrows and other embellishments: "One line represents the boundary," says scholar Wyatt MacGaffey, "the other is ambivalently both the path leading across the boundary, as to the cemetery; and the vertical path of power linking 'the above' with 'the below'.

This relationship, in turn, is polyvalent, since it refers to God and man, God and the dead, and the living and the dead." The Cosmogram was sometimes drawn on the ground or on a surface whereupon oaths or sacred objects were placed to be empowered, and the shape itself was added to other charms for their enhancement; for example, an x might be formed from pins to ritually seal shut a magical item.

In addition to images, writing could be a powerful method or addition to working a spell. Magical writing seems to be as old as writing itself; naturally, hoodoo absorbed some of this practice. Some magical inscriptions were in the form of specific "magic words" like the Sator Square (a European charm consisting of the words SATOR AREPO TENET OPERA ROTAS which was said to protect against disease and disasters) whereas others might be transcriptions of special prayers, or verses taken from sacred texts. The notion of using special "mystic alphabets" was also introduced by Cabblist influenced books like *The Key of Solomon* and *The Great Book of Magical Art*, but this practice seems to have been employed rarely if ever at all.

DANCES

A 1907 book charmingly entitled *The Negro: A Menace to American Civilization* proclaims: "A voodoo dance at its height would soon convince one that it is not necessary to go to Africa to meet with that species of negro moral degradation that passeth all understanding and of the depth of which there is no measuring." Unfortunately most pre-1920 accounts of these ceremonial dances seem to be of this type, not really giving much information other than complaining of how they appeared to be obscene. Since it seems these dances were usually communal in nature, and often would draw outsider's attention from the music and the largeness of the gathering, they are well documented in existing, but little reliable information about the purposes or the steps or styles of the dances can be found. They are possibly the most commonly referenced aspect of the historical practice of "Voodooism" and were apparently a favorite target of disparagement for those opposed to the art. John Q. Anderson,

writing on the subject of the dances, notes: "Unfortunately, the voodoo ceremonies had largely disappeared by the time journalists and writers became suffice-ently interested to leave descriptions."

An unnamed 19th century New York journalist, seeking to learn more about Voodoo practice, was informed that the Congo Dance was very similar, "*minus the scandalous features.*" His eyewitness account was quoted in *Mysteries and Miseries of America's Great Cities* (1883) as follows:

"It used to be given every Sunday ... There were large crowds there — black, brown and yellow. A dry-goods box and an old pork barrel formed the orchestra. These were beaten with sticks or bones, used like drumsticks so as to keep up a continuous rattle, while some old men and women chanted a song that appeared to be purely African ... The dance was certainly peculiar, and I observed that only a few old persons, who had probably all been slaves, knew how to dance it. The women did not move their feet from the ground. They only writhed their bodies and swayed in undulatory motions from ankle to waist — a great deal of what the French term *elles dehanchaient.* The men leaped and performed feats of gymnastic dancing which reminded me of some steps in the *jota Aragonesa.* Small bells were attached to their ankles." He remarked that nobody in attendance seemed to actually understand the meaning of the song lyrics being sung.

In the 1920s a man named Luke Turner, who claimed to be a nephew of the famous 19th century Voodoo Queen Marie Laveau, said of the dances she had hosted so famously: "She give [sic] the dance the first Friday night in each month and they have crab gumbo and rice to eat and the people dance." He claimed that the well-known "Voodoo Dances" of Congo Square and St. John's Eve were just parties, and that real hoodoo dances were always held in private. It's of note that Congo Square was first opened up for these spectacle dances in 1817 as a way for whites to monitor the content of slave's performances.

Turner's own performance of a private hoodoo dance, intended to drive away a man who was troubling one of his spell-seeking clients, is documented: At ten o'clock at night, nine wooden stakes were driven into the ground in his private courtyard. Nine black chickens were bound to the stakes — one chicken at each — by the left leg. A fire was built from nine sticks, each of which had the victim's name written on them. Four Thieves Vinegar was sprinkled over the ground. His assistant, Zora Neale Hurston, beat the ground with a stick and chanted the victim's name in rhythm, and then the dance began. "From the fire to the circle of fluttering chickens and back again to the fire. The feathers were picked from the heads of the chickens in the frenzy of the dance and scattered to the four winds. He called the victim's name each time as he whirled three times with the chicken's head-feathers in his hand, then he flung them far ... One by one the chickens were seized and killed by having their heads pulled off ... When the last fowl was dead, Turner drank a great draught of wine and sank before the altar. When he arose, we gathered some ashes from the fire and sprinkled the bodies of the dead chickens ... The spirits of the dead chickens had been instructed never to let the trouble-maker pass inward to New Orleans again after he had passed them going out." The spell was completed by Turner and his assistant depositing the carcasses of the chickens along the highway leading out of town, the intention being to drive the victim out of town the by the same path.

Turner was an old

man at the time that his performance was recorded, and if we assume he had not recently modified his techniques, then his method can be considered an indication of late 19th and early 20th century African-American ritual dance practices. Its function appears to be to raise and enhance energy, and it is only one element of a spell; in typical hoodoo work, the sacrifice of the chickens, the chanting, the burning of the name-sticks, and the ritual disposal of the carcasses could have been considered a whole spell in and of itself, without the addition of the dance.

LOCATIONS

"Of Places Wherein We May Conveniently Execute the Experiments and Operations of the Art.

"The places best fitted for exercising and accomplishing Magical Arts and Operations are those which are concealed, removed, and separated from the habitations of men. Wherefore desolate and uninhabited regions are most appropriate, such as the borders of lakes, forests, dark and obscure places, old and deserted houses, whither rarely and scarce ever men do come, mountains, caves, caverns, grottos, gardens, orchards; but best of all are cross-roads, and where four roads meet, during the depth and silence of night. But if thou canst not conveniently go unto any of these places, thy house, and even thine own chamber, or, indeed, any place, provided it hath been purified and consecrated with the necessary ceremonies, will

be found fit and convenient for the convocation and assembling of the Spirits."

So says Book Two of *The Key of Solomon* in the famous and infamous 1914 De Laurence edition.[+]

Traditional hoodoo conjure does not usually place so a great deal of emphasis on performing the magic in a special location as it does in laying the finished magic (which tends to be a physical talisman, potion or other material infused with power) in special locations. Works intended to influence a specific person are usually placed near to that person, or in a location related to the behavior desired from that person — for example, laying the work in a graveyard if the spell is intended to make them die. Rivers seem to be associated with the concept of *running,* and so are used either to drive or lead away (people or conditions), or to stimulate (as in spells where a person's hair secured in running river water will allegedly cause a headache.) "Public highways" are often mentioned as being used to hide or dispose of conjure charms, and crossroads in particular have a reputation worldwide as a place of mystery and potential evil. Spells meant to cause death or illness are often placed in graveyards.

[+] A loophole in international copyright laws of the time allowed the American L. W. de Laurence to pirate the British S. L. MacGregor Mathers's book, with De Laurence's own name pasted over that of Mathers in the text.

Old Time Spells

LOVE SPELLS

Love Powders, Potions and Herbs.

Love powders have been sold in Europe by apothecaries since at least the Middle Ages, and the standard pharmacies of New Orleans were recorded to still be stocking them as of 1917. One text claimed these premade mixtures were mostly favored by men. It would appear the pharmacists themselves did not always seem to believe in the power of such products and only sold them due to the popular demand. Numerous accounts indicate that drug store "love powders" were made up from whatever cheap or harmless preparation the pharmacist had on hand. Sweeteners were common bases; coloring might be added for effect.

Historians of folklore document that the genuine and traditional love powders were made in many different ways: A wooden cross taken from a grave, cut into small pieces and burnt to fine ashes, was one recipe for a love powder; such ashes would be carried while visiting the targeted person and speaking to them of love. Another recipe was made only from dried persimmon-bark, beaten fine. Leaves of the liverwort (possibly *umbilicus rupestris*, or else plants from the *hepatica* family which are known for their heart-shaped leaves) were said to draw love if dried before a fire and powdered, then sprinkled over a desired person's clothes Carrying the leaves of liverwort on the bosom additionally was said to attract suitors in abundance.

A person's own blood, dried along with the testicles of a hare and the liver of a dove and powdered, also was an old mixture for the purpose of drawing love; it was specified that the blood should be taken on a Friday in the spring and the mixture fed to the target of the user's affection. A "certain bone" (possibly a rib) taken from the grave of a preacher and powdered along with dirt from the head or foot of the same grave, and sprinkled on one's clothing, was another mixture to win a girl's affection. It was also said that elecampane, gathered at dawn on St. John's Eve, dried and powdered with ambergris and then carried for nine days over the heart then fed to the desired person, was another mixture for the purpose. A "modern" recipe for love powder was given in 1859 as two parts Spanish flies (cantharides) mixed with one part each musk, phosphorus and cloves. French Love Powder was made from 3 ounces powdered lodestone, 1 ounce "certain parts of fish", 2 ounces stinging nettle and 10 grains otto of rose.

A perfume recipe meant to secure a woman's love was to combine marrow from the left foot of a wolf with Chypre perfume powder and ambergris, and always wear the resulting ointment as a fragrance.

One recipe for a love potion, which was available to purchase by mail-order circa 1918, was as follows:

"Rx— Get a fresh egg and three leaves called young

man's love, and three leaves called young woman's love, and five hairs from a real black cat. Put into a pint jar and cover with strong vinegar. Touch three times a day with the right hand and say, 'This day compels you to love me,' and mention the name of the person you want. Stop at the end of the sixth day."

"Young Man's Love" and "Young Woman's Love" both seem to be names associated with the plant southernwood, though the usage, here at least, suggests that two different herbs are meant. Some other herbs and flowers used in love magic can be determined by their folk names. A partial list is as follows:

Heart's-Ease *(Viola tricolor)*

Kiss-Me-Quick *(Saxifraga umbrosa)*

Forget-Me-Not *(Ajuga chamaepitys)*

True Forget-Me-Not *(Myosotis scorpioides)*

Love-In-A-Mist *(Nigella damascena)*

Love-Bind *(Clematis vitalba)*

Love-Apples *(Lycopersicum esculentum)*

Love-Ache *(Levisticum officinale OR Ligusticum scoticum)*

Love-Me *(Myosotis palustris)*

Lover's-Links *(Umbilicus rupestris)*

Lover's-Pride *(Persicaria maculosa)*

Lover's-Steps *(Lolium temulentum)*

True-Love *(Paris quadrifolia)*

Lad-Love-Lass *(Artemisia abrotanum)*

Methods for employing these herbs might typically consist of including sprigs worked into bouquets which were presented to a lover, or mailing the flowers or leaves along with love letters. Many were also taken medicinally as aphrodisiacs. Those familiar with modern conjure formulas may also recognize a few of the names; one can presume that the plants originally were included in their namesake mixtures, or that the concoctions were at least intended to mimic their perfumes. For example, Cristiani's 1877 book of perfume recipes included the following one for Kiss-Me-Quick:

◆1 pint extract of jasmine, no. 1 (alcohol scented from first rinsing of jasmine pomade)
◆1/2 pint extract of violet, no. 2 (alcohol scented from second rinsing of violet pomade)
◆1/2 pint extract of rose, no. 2 (from rose pomade, as above)
◆1/4 pint tincture of vanilla
◆1/4 pint tincture of vetivert
◆1/2 pint tincture of orris
◆1/4 pint tincture of musk
◆1 ounce oil of bergamot
◆1 dram oil of rose
◆1 dram oil of cloves
◆8 ounces rosewater, double

Bodily Fluids.

A famous, and somewhat notorious, love charm used by women only was to add some of their monthly menstrual blood into the food or drink of the man they wished to snare. Men had their tactic as well: the *Petit Albert* indicates that feeding the woman semen will coerce her love in the same way.

Human and Animal Parts.

To cut off and carry the index finger from the right hand of a female corpse was a way for a man to attract women.

To acquire the little hooked bone from a toad was believed to hold much power in magic. In love spells it would be used to scratch the desired person, thereby "hooking" them romantically. The hippomane from a foal, dried, carried, and touched to the person desired, was also said to draw their love.

A spell suggested for a man to win a woman's permanent affection, was to take the tongue of a turtle-dove and place it in one's own mouth when kissing her: she would become deeply enamored and be unable to refuse any requests.

Talismans, Charms, Dolls, Gris-Gris, Etc.

Poppets or what are nowadays called Voodoo Dolls could be used in love magic. For love drawing one was instructed to make a wax image of a couple embracing, and smoke the figures in a mixture of amber and aloeswood incense, during the sixth mansion of the moon. To bring love and affection to a marriage and remove any malicious spells against the couple, the same spell was used but it was specified that the man should be formed in red wax and the woman in white, and that the work be done in the thirteenth mansion of the moon.

An old American Indian charm used by women was to create a small figure of a man whose love was desired, pierce a hole over the heart, and fill it with love powders while addressing the doll by name and bidding he requite her affection. Married women could forgo the doll and rub the powder directly on the chest of their sleeping husbands to induce fidelity and affection.

A spell suggested for winning a girl — and presumably just as effective for a boy — was to get some of her hair and combine it with sawdust scraped from a wood floor. It would be placed in a bottle and wrapped in cloth, then the bottle stored in one's bedroom or buried in the ground near one's home or hangout.

A sort of love mojo was described as being used amongst certain American Indian women: it was made from a "thimble" (in this instance probably meaning a small leather pouch) filled with powder of mica and vermillion, along with a piece of the man's hair or clothing or a clipping from his fingernail, and was worn around the woman's neck.

Another such charm bag of the 19th century for drawing a woman's love was documented as being made from pepper, wool, three castor beans and rusty iron wrapped in cloth, tied with two hairs from a male horse and one from a female, and soaked with whiskey. It is remarkable that many of these ingredients would nowadays be considered to have powers of anti-love in hoodoo tradition. The old account of this bag does not explain the maker's logic, but it is possible it could have been meant particularly to drive away rivals or to enhance the wearer's manliness (pepper and iron being associated with Mars in European magic, and in African Yoruba magic with the warrior orisha, Ogun.)

A spell, part mojo part love powder, for drawing a woman's love, was for the man to take her sock or stocking, cut it into fine strips, put it into the bag and then urinate upon it. After letting it dry, he would burn it to ash and sneak these ashes into the woman's food or drink, to ensure she could love no one else.

To take the freshly worn shoes of the desired person and tie your own shoes up inside them was another old trick for love — though for reasons of foot-size, a woman would probably have an easier time than a man at performing the job. Another shoe spell was to add some hair from the desired person into your own shoe before wearing it.

A type of bottle spell for love was made by putting into a small jar or bottle lodestone, Adam and Eve root, and Hoyt's Cologne. This informant notes that the original worker whose methods he was reporting, may have mixed the cologne with additional ingredients. If the jar were made properly, the roots would continue to grow — and presumably, so would the love.

The Petit Albert, a book favored by French speakers and especially around the New Orleans area, gives a spell for The

Apple of Love: "You go one Friday morning before sunrise into a fruit orchard, and pick from a tree the most beautiful apple that you can; then you write with your own blood on a bit of white paper your first and last name, and on another line following, the first and last name of the person by whom you would like to be loved, and you try to have three of her hairs, to which you affix three of yours which you shall use to bind the little message you have written with another one, the which is to have nothing but the word *Scheva,* likewise written in your blood, then you slice the apple in two, you throw away the seeds, and in their place you lay your papers bound with hair, and with two sharp skewers made from green myrtle branches, you neatly rejoin the apple's two halves and you will put it to dry in an oven, ensuring that it grows hard and free of moisture like the dried apples of Lent; you wrap it thereafter in the leaves of bay and myrtle, and endeavor to place it under the mattress of the bed or the cot of the beloved person, without letting her know of it, and in a short while she will give unto you some sign of her love."

Fidelity.

To ensure a woman's fidelity, a man could wipe up both his and her genitals, after coitus, with his own sock. Doing this three times would cause any other man to be unable to perform with her. Another fidelity cure was to take red ants and fry them in grease. This grease, strained, could then be used to anoint the genitals of the woman and likewise would prevent any other man from maintaining his erection with her. Another trick was for the man to coat his male member with honey and dust it with the woman's own hair very finely chopped, before intercourse; this would result in the woman growing disinterested in sex altogether, until such time as the trick was reversed by repeating the procedure but with the man replacing his own hair for the woman's and adding a bit of civet to the mix. Marrow from the spine of a wolf, fed to the woman, would also put an end to her running around.

To ensure a man's fidelity, a woman could take a small piece of cloth cut from the underwear of the man she wished to hold; "about as big as a dollah bill." This scrap would then be soaked for three nights in her own urine, after which she would take the cloth and hold it to her vulva and would trace the shape onto the cloth. She would then tack the cloth underneath her mattress, on the side of the bed where she sleeps, to ensure the man would be submissive to her. Another more extreme spell used to prevent a man from functioning sexually at all was to take the penis of a wolf and a piece of white thread, then come near to the man being targeted. One would call his name, and at the moment of his reply, a loop would be tied around the wolf's penis. This would render the man impotent.

A person's foot-track could be used to draw their love or to hold their fidelity. The track had to be scraped up from the heel to the toe and the dust kept for as long as the person's presence was wished.

An old New Orleans gris-gris for bringing on a marriage was made by carrying a small metal case with a picture of St. Joseph.

Candle Magic.

By the 1910s, candle magic was in use. Blue candles were the color most favored for love and fidelity matters. Pink was also used for love only. White candles were used for bringing marriages.

Removing Rivals.

Sometimes a person felt confident they could succeed with the man or woman if their dreams if only a competitor were put out of the way. To remove a love rival, one could draw a portrait of the said competitor in the dirt, climb up a tree, and with a gun shoot the portrait in the heart. Another way, attributed to Marie Laveau, was to take a lemon, and cut a slit into it which one filled with cayenne pepper, "coprus root", gunpowder, and a paper on which the rival's name was written nine times with an X over each transcription, and your own wish for them to move on written underneath. The lemon would then be pinned shut with nine pins arranged to make three X shapes. This lemon would be buried at the foot of a grave of a person who "died bad." Another way to make the rival leave town was through foot track magic: their footprint could be lifted from the dirt, scraped up toe to heel, and then the dust tossed into a river. Breaking up a marriage could be achieved by placing a file (presumably of steel or iron) under the steps of the house.

To Return a Lost Lover.

The professional hoodoo of modern times tends to find return lover spells amongst the most common requests. This evidently was not so in the past; or at least, such spells are not nearly so well documented. For this kind of trouble, the following remedies were suggested:

Write the targeted person's name nine times on a newspaper, fold it up and bury it under the doorstep of the house. As the paper dissolves in the dirt, the person's mind will grow more obsessed with the notion of coming home.

Get a photograph of the person and write on the back of it his name three times while declaring "You must return" at each; and then write the name of the person who wants him back three times. The sets of names should intersect into an X shape. Then take a mirror — the informant specifies it be one set over a mantelpiece — and remove the backing so as to slip the photograph inside so it will be facing the glass. Replace the mirror over the mantle, and in front of it burn a blue candle for two hours a day at the same time each day, and always pinch out the candle instead of blowing it out.

The targeted person's hair, placed in a bottle of rainwater set near the door, also calls the person to the home. This could also be used to attract any person to come visit.

MONEY SPELLS

The traditional users of hoodoo were probably not the sort of people who expected to ever attain immense wealth and live amongst the upper classes of society. For this reason, old time money spells more commonly amount to gambling spells, treasure hunting spells or business improvement spells: these, it can be assumed, were felt to be the most likely ways a person could come by unexpected cash or improve standing in their own little community. Some folks dislike the suggestion that old-time hoodoo practitioners (that is, they tend to assume, blacks) were so particularly inclined to gamble, as it calls to mind certain negative stereotypes of the past; but it's not too different from the phenomenon seen nowadays amongst low-income people of all races, who with an alarming frequency truly believe that winning the lottery is going to be their best chance to grow rich.

Gambling Talismans, Charms, Gris-Gris, Etc.

An old spell said to assure winnings at games of skill or chance was to first acquire an eel which died from lack of water, and skin it. Into the said skin one should put the gall of a bull who was killed by dogs, and a dram of vulture's blood. The skin would then be bound at both ends with a rope which had been used for an execution by hanging, and this whole mess was then put into a smokehouse for a fortnight, after which it was dried in an oven fueled with ferns which had to have been gathered on St. John's Eve. Onto the resulting object one was to write with his own blood, using a raven's feather for a quill, HVTY. The final creation was to be worn as a bracelet whenever gaming. A simpler device for the same purpose, said to make one "win every game one engages in" was to use a red silk string to tie a bat's heart to the right arm.

Skin of a black snake worn on the wrist, or skin of a cat worn about the neck, were lucky for gambling.

A gambling hand reputed to be from Doctor Buzzard's recipe, was to take a small pebble of lodestone, a small piece of John the Conqueror root and some Sampson snakeroot together with a suitable Psalm written out in yellow colored pencil. These would be set on a piece of red flannel which would be wrapped with the cloth pulled towards yourself, and your wish made aloud at each fold of the cloth. Once it was wrapped as small and tight as possible, the cloth was stitched in place, blessed, and dressed with Nightwood oil.

A gambler's lucky charm that, depending on your view, could be less or more complicated than a mojo hand, was to wear the hair of a suicide victim on one's own body for enhanced fortune. The spirits of those who "died bad" were generally felt to be the best aids to conjure (see earlier section about the Dead.) Similarly, the same old text reports, "There is a superstition at Monte Carlo that immediately after a suicide, all those playing against the bank will win."

Another trick for gambling reported in the *Encyclopaedia of Superstitions* is: "Money carried for three days in a man's shoe or a woman's stocking, can be invested in any gambling game with absolute surety of its winning powers."

Albertus Magnus says that to gain money, one should find a swallow's nest full of eggs; the eggs should be taken and boiled, then returned to the nest. The parent swallow then might bring a root into the nest, and if it does, "take it, put it into your purse, and carry it in your pocket, and be happy." It's notable that "purse" at this point in time would mean a cloth or leather bag similar to what are now used for mojo hands.

For Success in Business.
A charm for business was made with grave dirt and silver money wrapped in tinfoil, then folded toward one's self while making your wishes "In the name of the Lord."

To make a person rise in business and success, one would take a drawing of the person and cram it into the barrel of a muzzleloader gun with the usual amount of gunpowder needed to fire it; then the gun would be fired toward the sunrise.

For special money luck and business success, one could go to the grave of a noted gambler three days after his death and dig down to reach the body. After telling the deadman that he was being taken for success, one would take the thumb or the middle finger or the little finger from his left hand (in other words, the odd numbered fingers) and then soak it in alcohol for about a month. Once prepared, it would be sewn into a mojo bag and carried. A woman who performed this around 1907 was noted to have had exceptional luck purchasing and profiting from real estate. Knee bones and toe bones from dead men are also noted to have been thought lucky for gambling.

A charm for success at selling goods was to create a seal in silver, bearing an image of a man sitting on a chair and holding a balance in his hand. It was to be made in the sixteenth mansion of the moon and smoked in an incense of "well-smelling spices." Another way for the same intent was to take a twig from a switch that had been used to beat someone, and make it into a finger-ring wrapped with red silk. Wearing this ring would ensure customers would buy your goods at whatever price you asked.

Scrubbing the face first thing every morning with sugar was said to bring "good success" to a person.

Burning *Temple Incense* in one's home or business reputedly "drives out bad influences and helps one to succeed in all undertakings."

To attract customers, one could scrub the floor of the business with strong lye, but one had to do so in total silence. Another way was to scrub the establishment with the water left over after performing the famous Black Cat ritual: to this was added sugar and the oils of cinnamon and bergamot.

A spell used specifically by prostitutes for drawing clients was to bathe in water to which Hoyt's cologne, allspice, cinnamon and cloves had been added. Another way was to intentionally apply pubic lice to the genitals, which was said to draw clients; washing with tobacco would remove them.

For Money in General.

A general money wish could be fulfilled by St. Raymond if he were given a green candle, parsley and green onions each day for a set number of days (three, seven or nine, whichever the practitioner felt best) while repeating the wish.

Another hand for money drawing was made with sandbur, Sampson snakeroot and devil's shoestring to represent "Father, Son and Holy Ghost." They were wrapped in black cloth which was folded towards one's self, sewn in place with white thread, then kept in a red flannel bag. It was fed with whiskey or with camphor spirits. It is of note that modern hoodoo would consider most of these ingredients to be of a protective nature: perhaps the charm was particularly intended to protect against others interfering with one's money luck.

For general luck with money and for "finding something" every day, a spell from the *Petit Albert* required one find a root of English mandrake in the approximate shape of a human: "One will take it from the ground on a Monday in the springtime, when the

Moon is in a favorable sign, being in conjunction with Jupiter, in agreeable aspect with Venus." The root was then to be taken to a graveyard and buried on the plot of a grave, and watered for a month every day before sunrise with milk in which three bats had been drowned. At the end of the month the root would be retrieved — hopefully having grown larger during its sojourn — and was then to be dried in an oven fueled with vervain, and finally wrapped in a dead man's shroud. "As long as one is in possession of this mysterious root," says the *Albert*, "one is lucky — inclined to find things in the street, to succeed at games of chance, or by business; so much that one sees his wealth grow every day."

For a Job.

Spells for job-getting were also occasionally to be found. To win a job, nine drops of bloodroot oil were rubbed on the applicant's hands and the 27th psalm read (aloud or not, it is unclear) just before going to interview or apply. The old trick recommended by the Pennsylvania Dutchman John George Hohman, of carrying cinquefoil when asking for anything, may also have come in handy for this — according to tradition, anything would be granted if you asked for it while carrying cinquefoil.

CRIMINAL, COURT AND LAW SPELLS

For Victory in Court.

To win any just cause in court, one was advised to take a large sage leaf and write the names of the twelve apostles upon it, then wear it in one's shoe during court. (It's of note that this spell dates to an era when court cases rarely lasted more than a single day, so only one leaf was needed.) A spell from the same source, "to be used when you are standing before a court in your right, and the judge not being favorably disposed toward you," was to carry a paper on which was written JESUS NAZARENUS, REX JUDEORUM and on the way to court to recite "I (name) appear before the house of the Judge. Three dead men look out of the window; one having no tongue, the other having no lungs, and the third was sick, blind and dumb."

Another spell to assure winning in court if you were in the right, would be to take skunk cabbage during August, while the sun is in the constellation of Leo, and wrap it in a bay leaf and a dandelion, and carry this on your person.

To win a judge's favor, the judge's name was written nine times on a white candle, then turned upside down and run under water from a hydrant. The candle would then be burnt in its customary upright position, in a white saucer over a paper with the judge's name and surrounded with white sugar. The following prayer was to accompany: "In the name of the father, don't let Judge

_____ be against me, let him be for me and turn me loose when I get there." Then one would turn on the home hydrant before setting out to court, and recite: "In the name of the father, son and holy ghost, I'm going away from here, let me come back like I was going." The specification of white candle, sugar and saucer may come from the assumption that the judge will be white-skinned, for other sweetener-based spells of the period frequently specify similar instructions about matching the skin color of the target to the colors of the materials used.

Another spell to win in court or escape a conviction was to boil a buzzard and collect the grease produced. A live, small bird would be caught and rubbed with this buzzard-grease, then dusted with a mixture of grave dirt, ashes from a wooden grave marker, and love powder. The bird would be given instructions as to the desired outcome of the case, and then released inside the courtroom during trial. This spell is said to replace an older working wherein a live buzzard would be released into the room — a smaller bird, obviously, would be easier to smuggle inside without drawing attention, and the buzzard-grease provides it with equal power.

To get out of legal trouble, one took powdered Jack-in-the-pulpit and dressed his own body with it, then mixed a bit more of this powder with quicksilver which then was to be scattered in front of the courthouse. Another way was to heat splinters of lightning-struck wood in a skillet and touch them with a match, and let them burn down to ash. The ash would be scattered in front of the door of the courthouse early in the morning before anyone else had arrived; the person performing this spell was also instructed that the night before trial, he should go outdoors and look at the moon but not say any words while doing so.

To secure an acquittal, a person would rub a rabbit's foot and a raccoon's foot on the neck before court.

Avoiding Capture and Escaping the Law.

To keep out of jail, a red flannel mojo bag filled with quicksilver (in this case possibly meaning tinfoil) was carried. To get out of jail once one was already imprisoned, a person was instructed to snip a bit of his pubic hair off every day and let it fall to the floor of the cell. When the cell would be cleaned, the hair would be swept out and, by the power of sympathy, the rest of one's body would surely follow.

To escape the law after committing a crime, a criminal was advised to make a powder of garlic and gunpowder, and sprinkle this in his tracks while fleeing. He should then try to cross a body of water and throw down some of this powder at the first step before passing through, and at the first step out after crossing over. Another way to escape was to carry dried and powdered cow manure, and after doing the crime, grease his shoes or feet and coat them heavily with this powder; the same could be done with a dried and powdered horny-toad in place of the manure.

A spell against a watchdog, to make it sleep through one's coming and going, was to take a stick and make a "scratch" in it, and plant it into the ground near the dog.

To steal without being caught, one should grease up his hands with snake oil acquired from a snake that was caught in a graveyard. "Nobody will see yer, an' yer won't git found out."

A charm created to allow one to commit crimes and never be captured was made from a genuine black cat bone, wrapped in the bark of the plant from which John the Conqueror root is had, then thoroughly bound up in black cord to make a type of jack-ball. This was dressed with Nightwood oil and empowered with psalms recited over it, and finally blessed.

An old spell originally used with the intent to help a slave avoid punishment from his master, used a powder made from cow dung, red pepper and white-people's hair, scorched and then reduced to a powder, and sprinkled in the master's bedroom.

A very famous old spell, said to be used by thieves, was the Hand of Glory. This was a dead man's hand (preferably a hanged man), severed from the body, wrapped in a piece of funeral shroud and put to cure in a clay pot along with green vitriol, saltpeter, salt, and long pepper, for two weeks. It then was removed and dried in the sun. Into the hand was set a candle made from fat of a hanged man, virgin wax, and a mysterious ingredient called *sisame de Laponie* (literally "Sesame of Lapland" — a nonsensical term.) If one could successfully assemble these goods and leave this candle to burn in any house while robbing it, it would cause the residents to either fall into the deepest sleep, or would freeze them in place until the candle was put out. An alternative to the impossible Hand of Glory was made from four ounces of the herb serpentine, shut into an earthenware pot and left in a continually warm spot (such as inside of a dung heap) for two weeks. The herbs would supposedly transform into "worms" from which an oil could be extracted, and this oil could be used to fuel a lamp which would produce the same effects as the Hand of Glory.

Detecting Criminals and Correcting Misdeeds.

To find out a murderer, the murdered person should be buried with an egg in each hand and two pins between her lips. "That will bring her murderer back."

There are several spells in existence alleged to be effective for the retrieving of stolen goods:

To force a thief to return stolen goods: take three coffin nails, oiled with the fat of a hanged man. Before sunrise, go to a pear tree and recite: "Oh, thief, I bind you by the first nail, which I drive into thy skull and thy brain, to return the goods thou hast stolen to their former place; thou shalt feel as sick and as anxious to see me, and to see the place you stole from, as felt the disciple Judas after betraying Jesus. I bind thee by the other nail, which I drive into your lungs and liver, to return the stolen goods to their former place; thou shall feel as sick and as anxious to see me, and to see the place you have stolen from, as did Pilate in the fires of hell. The third nail I shall drive into thy foot, oh thief, in order that thou shalt return the stolen goods to the very same place from which thou hast stolen them. Oh, thief, I bind thee and compel thee, by the three holy nails which were driven through the hands and feet of Jesus Christ, to return the stolen goods to the very same place from which thou hast stolen them. In the name of the father, the son and the holy spirit." It is not expressly stated, but one can infer the nails are supposed to be driven into the tree at the relevant points in the chant.

Another way to force the return of stolen items, is to take three small pinches of salt, three crumbs of bread and three tiny portions of lard. Build a large fire and strew these items upon it, and speak the following three times:

"I lay for the thief, bread salt and lard,
Upon the flame, for thy sin is hard.
I lay it upon thy lung, liver and heart,
That thou may feel a bitter smart.
It shall come upon thee, need and dread,
As it approaches a dire death.

All veins shall in thy
body burst,
And cause thee pain and
quenchless thirst,
That thou shalt have no
peace or rest,
Till all the theft thou
hast returned,
And place it where thou
hast taken the
plunder,
Or be caught by lightning
and thunder.
In the name of the father,
the son and the holy
spirit."

Still another method is
the following, from *Pow-
Wows or The Long Lost
Friend:* "Walk out early
in the morning before
sunrise, to a juniper-tree,
and bend it with the left
hand toward the rising
sun, while you are saying:
'Juniper-tree, I shall bend
and squeeze thee, until
the thief has returned the
stolen goods to the place
from which he took
them.' Then you must
take a stone and put it on
the bush, and under the
bush and the stone you
must place the skull of a
malefactor ... Yet you
must be careful, in case
the thief returns the
stolen goods, to unloose
the bush and replace the
stone where it was
before." This should all be
done, as with the previous
methods, "In the name of
the father, the son and
the holy spirit."

JINX, HARM AND DEATH SPELLS

In the minds of many, the terms "hoodoo" and "witchcraft" produce images of wicked sorcerers conjuring up evil spells meant to harm and kill. The misunderstanding that hoodoo is a purely malicious form of magic causes many period texts to attribute harmful intentions to workings that do not sound, by their descriptions, to have been anything of the sort. One notable example was a mojo bag that was made with a rabbit's foot and a pair of dice, but was described as an evil charm intended to drive someone mad: the actual ingredients would ind- icate that the worst thing someone could get off such a bag is gambling fever. Many of the old accounts of harmful tricks come from people who found the charms on their property or in the possession of others, rather than from the original makers or purchasers of the items, and so the informants might not have genuinely understood what had been discovered. I've tried to omit any "tricks" that sounded like obvious mistakes (but I can't quite promise that a few didn't unknowingly work their way in.)

Death Spells.

Collect some spittle from the victim. One hollows out a piece of wild parsnip root to form a tube, and into it puts the spit, seven earthworms beaten into paste, and seven splinters of wood from a lightning-struck tree. Take this tube to another lightning-struck tree: dig a hole at the tree's base and bury first a slab of yellow stone, on top of which place the tube plus seven yellow pebbles (yellow here representing trouble.) Fill in the hole. Build a fire over the spot to "destroy all traces of [the] work." The practitioner and client should both fast after doing this. If properly carried out, the victim will die within seven days.

To stop up someone's bowels and make them sick unto death, collect some of the victim's dung and put it into a container that seals with a cork or other stopper. Bury this stopped container at the corner of the victim's house.

A person's tintype photo, turned upside down and hidden in a place where it couldn't be disturbed, would cause the person in the photo to die. Another way to kill was to write the victim's name nine times on paper, wrap it in white cloth, and squirt it with milk from the udder of a black cow. One then placed it with "bad herbs" (i.e. those traditionally used for malicious intent) before rolling it up, tying nine knots around it, and burying it on the grave of someone who died bad. The dead man should be provided an offering of whiskey as payment for his assistance.

To kill another way, a brown egg with the victim's name written on it is placed under said victim's doorstep. The egg can also be hollowed and the name written on paper hidden inside.

Illness and Misfortune. To cause illness and madness in someone, one would take a piece of hair from the person, bind it in cord and bury it in the victim's family's plot in the graveyard, under a brick. Another way to achieve the same was to fill a bottle with new pins, new needles and new nails along with the victim's hair and wrap it all in red flannel; or a similar rite used a bottle with nine new pins and nine new needles along with the victim's hair, and the charm was buried under the victim's doorstep.

To cause headaches, one could place the victim's hair into flowing water, such as a stream or brook. For this working, the hair should be secured in some way, such as being wedged between two stones.

To bring harm to a magical enemy "so that she receives pock marks over her entire body," one would take butter from one's own house and melt it in an iron pan till boiling. Wintergreen or ivy would be fried in this, and then three coffin nails driven into the resulting sauce. The whole mixture would be hidden in a dark place, with the result that "the witch will be sick for half a year." There is no instruction to name the enemy at any point — perhaps it is meant to be used when the trouble-maker is unknown.

To discreetly afflict someone with harmful conjure, one's own hands could be dusted with graveyard dirt and the intended victim touched in some normal manner, as by a handshake. This would put upon him all the harmful properties of grave dirt such as sickness, sluggishness and possible death.

A charm to cause pain was made from pins and needles stuck into a piece of cloth. The source does not reveal what kind of cloth — presumably it would be a scrap of clothing from the victim, but the mystical red flannel is another possibility.

Charles Godfrey Leland records the following "Etruscan" spells which even he notes to bear a resemblance to traditional hoodoo practice (and well he should, since several of these ingredients don't even natively grow in Italy): "Take a toad. Obtain some of the hairs of your victim. Tie them to the left leg of the toad, and put the animal into a covered pot. As it suffers the enemy will suffer, when it dies he will die. But if he is only to suffer and not die, remove the hair from the leg of the toad and let it go." ... "To put misfortune (*il male auguro*) into a house, so that all things may go wrong, take a black cat and cut away all its skin, for so much as it suffers so much will the person suffer whom you would bewitch. And letting the cat go, say: *"Ti ho tagliato il pelo, Perche tu mandi alla malora ___."* ("I have cut the skin from thee That thou shalt carry misery to ___.') Then name the one whom you wish to suffer. Then take the skin or hair, with nettles, skins of Indian figs with the prickles [*Opuntia vulgaris*], powdered horse scrapings, pepper, wild chestnuts, carrots, and garlic, and with these the hairs of the person, and pulverise all very finely (*fine, fine, che sia*

possibile). Then take linseed and hempseed, seeds of melons and pumpkins, and put them all in a black glazed pot, which place on the hole of a privy. Then take two candles tied with black and red thread, and let it remain for three days, first lighting the candles, and as soon as they are burned out renew them. And when three days are passed, then, exactly at midnight, put the pot on the fire, and say:—
"Non faccio bollire questa pentola,
Ma faccio bollire il corpo e l'anima
Di. . . .'
("It is not this pot which I boil,
But I boil the body and soul
Of . . .')
"This liquid is then put into a small bottle, and thrown into the house of the one to whom you wish harm, and from that time that person will have no peace."

A European spell, printed by The American publisher L.W. De Laurence, "For the destruction of some body," said that one would make an image of a man with a front and back face (a Janus) during the twenty first mansion of the moon, and smoke it with an incense of jet and sulfur. The image would then be placed in a brass box along with more jet and sulfur, plus some hair taken from the person to be victimized by this spell.

To jinx a house, so that no one will move into it or so those who are in it will have bad luck, get an old shoe and take it to the hearth of the fireplace. Turn the shoe upside down and secure it up the chimney with a ten-penny nail. After this, make nine cross marks up the chimney with chalk, and in each of the four corners of the house.

To "run one crazy" or cause insanity, the victim's hair would be taken and tied around a new ten-penny nail. The nail would then be buried head-down under the victim's doorstep. Another way was to take the victim's hair and place it into a slit made through the bark of a tree. As the bark would grow back over it, the person's sanity would be lost.

An evil mojo could be fashioned from red clover, sulfur, powdered glass, and either red flannel or the red seeds of Jack-in-the-pulpit. It was to be wrapped in skin cut from a live cat. A type of mojo made with grave dirt, "nightshade root" (possibly meaning poke root in this case) and devil's snuff and hidden on a victim's property or in the path where he would walk, would bring harm and bad luck. A bottle filled with nails, red flannel and whiskey, likewise set in one's path, was another way to bring misfortune.

Needles, pins, snake heads and the victim's hair could be combined all together in a bag to do harm. Similarly, to harm but not kill, a mojo could be made in red flannel, filled with snakeroot, needles and pins wrapped in the hair of the victim.

To feed a person grave dirt or to sprinkle it around his property would cause illness.

Live Things.
Sickness by "live things" was a commonly reported

ailment caused by witchcraft. The witch would use some method to fill the victim's body with animals or animal parts which would then continue to grow inside them as living animals, and cause a variety of health problems. Ways to do this included feeding the victim powdered parts of animals such as snakes, toads, lizards, or other unpleasant creatures; sneaking a piece of hair into a victim's drink was another popular method, for the hair was believed to then transform into a worm or a snake after being consumed. A more complicated mixture was made from pulverizing toad's heads, scorpion's heads, hair, nine needles and nine pins and mixing it into the food of the unlucky person. If the victim's food could not be accessed, a bottle filled with reptile claws and horsehair buried under the victim's door was said to bring the same fate.

The Voodoo Doll.

For most folks, the poppet or "Voodoo doll" is the most common image that springs to mind when it comes to the topic of harmful magic and witchcraft. A record of a doll to make someone crazy consists of a black doll pierced with pins and needles (in the head region?), put into a container, and buried outside of the intended victim's property. Some said the dolls could be made from snake oil mixed with flour or sand, the figure then named for the victim, and then baked by a fire before being stuck with pins by the practitioner. The location of the pin's insertion would cause pains in the victim's corresponding body parts;

but a pin stuck in the
heart would kill the
victim dead. Another
source specified dolls
should be made of
beeswax or of mud from a
crawfish's hole, named by
the practitioner, and then
pierced with a thorn in
order to create various
afflictions dependent
upon where the thorn is
put. Coating the doll in
blood is also mentioned,
instead of piercing with
pins.

PROTECTION and JINX-REMOVAL

In the historical sources, blacks and whites alike complain that as a culture, African-Americans had a tendency to attribute any kind of misfortune to being brought on them by the work of malicious witchcraft. Because of this, there was some overlap between such spells as were meant to remove or protect against conjure, and those which were meant to bring good luck: the philosophy seemed to be that, without the negative influence of harmful magic, a person should be happy and lucky at all times.

Baths.

Just as one could wash away physical dirt and germs with proper bathing techniques, it was believed one could also wash away spiritual uncleanliness and supernatural ills by using special washes. A bath for removing an evil spell could be made from a mixture of salt, red pepper and silver coins added to the washing water. Bathing in an infusion of pokeberry root also would do the same. Salt, pepper and urine mixed together was another wash said to remove evil.

Afflicted limbs could be washed in a mixture of saltpeter, washing soda and vinegar to cure the magic.

A cure for "lost nature" (impotence) was done with a new package each of dry mustard powder, saltpeter and baking soda. Pour the soda into one gallon of water "in the name of the father," the saltpeter "in the name of the son," and the mustard "in the holy spirit." Then continue to conjure: "Remove these evil spirits from the person's body." The mixture was then used as a wash. This was performed on Mondays, Wednesdays and Fridays.

A girl who was afflicted with the conjure of Live Things, was cured by bathing "in an infusion of mullein and moss made with boiling water in a tub. After the bath the water was thrown toward the sunset and this line repeated: 'As the sun sets in the west so should the works of the Devil end in judgment.'"

Protection from Evil. Branding a horse-shoe into the wood of the front door would keep away any jinxes from the house.

An old shoe placed with three pins and three needles into a cloth and sewn up together would protect the house if the resulting bundle was kept inside.

To fasten sea-onion over the primary entry of one's house ensured no witchcraft would trouble the inhabitants. The same source states that if one is already troubled by a witch, one should sweep the floor and save the sweepings in a pile for three days. On the third day it should be covered with a black drill cloth, then one would take the stick of an elm tree and "flog the dirt heap bravely." The witch would be forced to stop working or else be battered to death through sympathetic magic.

Both the rabbit's foot and the famous black cat bone curios, mentioned elsewhere in this book, had the reputation to keep off conjure if carried.

Strings of hexagonal blue glass beads were worn on the body to protect from witchcraft or the evil eye. These "charm strings" were especially worn by women and children. Black glass beads could also be worn to guard against health troubles. Silver coins — especially silver dimes — could be drilled and strung to make protective jewelry as well.

Eating three garlic cloves on St. Martin's Eve would protect one from any witchcraft.

To carry any of the following charms would preserve the bearer against any jinxes or harmful spells: John the Conqueror root, rabbit's foot, or the luck stones called "fairy crosses."

Tying red flannel strings around the ankles, knees and arms would also keep off conjure.

Carrying the small, round, hollow bone of a ham keeps off evil eye.

A sprinkling powder of red pepper and salt could be used to keep away and negate evil spells. Another similar powder was made from red pepper and sulfur.

Removing Witchcraft and Conjure.

Three branches each rue, hazelnut and juniper, burned as fumigation, will purify a space. Burning *Temple Incense* will do the same.

Sprinkling red pepper in one's shoes or dropping silver coins into the shoes before putting them on, would keep one from being conjured.

To remove a spell: at an odd-numbered hour, such as 7 o'clock, 9 o'clock, 11 o'clock, etc. write this formula and hang it on a string from the neck of the person or animal afflicted by black magic:

+IN+RI+
SATOR
AREPO
TENET
OPERA
ROTAS
C+M+B+

"And then proceed at once up into your house, cut or file on the spars so that it becomes like flour, and take three pinches of wheat flour and of salt. Give all of these articles mixed, to the person or cattle in the three highest name." [sic.] This will cause the person who cast the spell to appear, presumably to then be dealt with by more mundane methods.

If a spirit haunted a place, sprinkling holy water in the room would drive him off. Reading backwards from the Bible would do the same.

A method for using grave dirt to remove a curse was done by taking some of the dirt from the freshest grave in the cemetery. It would be kept in one's pocket till all the dirt "wasted away." It is of note that at the time of this spell (1867) a "pocket" might be a separate item from the rest of one's clothing, taking the form of a cloth pouch, similar to a modern style mojo bag, that was worn under the garment rather than sewn into it. Clothes were sometimes made with slits in order to facilitate use of the separate pockets.

To cure "fits" brought by conjure, one could make a pone of cornbread using the bath water of the afflicted person, and mixing into it his powdered hair and fingernail clippings. After baking, the bread would be wrapped in some unwashed clothing belonging to the afflicted and the whole bundle thrown into a river on the dark of the moon at midnight.

A potion that was imbibed to remove evil was made from blackroot and red oak bark mixed with alum and bluestone: it was said it would make one vomit back up the magical "poison" that had caused the harm. Powdered scorpion mixed with whiskey was another beverage said to remove conjure. Yet another, possibly more pleasant mixture, was made from filing pieces of silver into a glass of water to drink. Remarkably, it seems that a proxy could do this version on behalf of the afflicted: a man admitted to undertaking this cure for his bewitched brother, in 1894.

To rub the body with bloodroot or with a fish-bone was said to remove conjure.

One could cure conjure by cutting open a living black hen and binding it to the victim's feet.

A stomach-plaster to cure a bewitched child could be made as follows: pound together almond oil, deer's tallow, rose vinegar (vinegar in which rose petals have been soaked), and caraway seed. The resulting mash should be placed upon a blue paper and laid on the child's stomach.

Swallowing a small piece of silver was said to cure conjure, as the evil would stick to the metal and pass out of the body.

If any bewitched item were found — that is to say, the item that was used to cause the jinx — it could be picked up with a piece of paper (so as not to touch the item directly) and thrown into a body of water, then salt sprinkled in all areas where the trick had been in contact. Tricked items were considered to have "germs" according to this informant.

Another way of dealing with a found trick was to place it into a mojo bag with yeast powder and lodestone, then chuck the whole charm into a river: this would cure the witchcraft from the victim and send it back to the person who created it.

Burning anything that has been affected by witchcraft or had been used to bring it on is a classic remedy for jinxes. In some versions it is believed that it will also do harm back to the person who caused the evil. One record states that the burning needs to be done between midnight and 1 AM.

MISCELLANEOUS

A piece of eelskin, a piece of brimstone and an Indian head penny sewn up together in a piece of velvet would protect the bearer and bring luck to him.

A "Bo' Dollar" (a large silver dollar) carried would bring good luck; to carry two was said to be even better.

Eating snake meat was said to make a hoodoo practitioner wise and intelligent.

A gambler having poor luck despite being in possession of some talisman or charm for the enhancement of his winnings, was said to be able to turn his luck from bad to good by switching the talisman from one pocket to the other. If this still didn't work, laying it on the table with his money would surely do the trick.

A rope that was used to hang someone is said to bring luck to the person who keeps it. The final object touched by a man before his being hanged also was considered to possess special luck.

Equal parts alum, sulfur, salt and John the Conqueror root (in this case named as being Jack-in-the-Pulpit root) can be combined to make a "lucky jack" or type of mojo bag.

Another lucky bag can be made as follows: "Take a little red bag, and sew it with red woollen thread — not with silk or cotton; the bag, too, must be of woollen, and of coarse cloth, and while sewing it, sing: — [Here the source gives a rustic

Italian charm that translates: "I sew this little bag for the good fortune of myself and of my family, and so as to hold far at bay misfortunes as well as disease."] Then take a crumb (*midolla*) of bread, and a little coarse salt, a sprig of rue, and some cummin, [sic] and keep repeating, while making it up, the same charm. And when made, the charm must always be borne on the same person, by night as well as by day."

Bibliography

WEB

"Barakat Gallery Store." The Barakat Gallery. Barakat, Inc. 6 Mar. 2012. ‹www.barakatgallery.com/store/Index.cfm/FuseAction/ItemDetails/UserID/0/CFID/39803792/CFTOKEN/34f51b2e5c7426f0-7C4D5AA5-3048-33BC-FC67DB9C101B2106/jsessionid/8430216fe883a75465f96464643 57c5a9432/ItemID/24669.htm›

"Cannibalism and the Witches Potion « All in the Past." All in the Past. 29 June 2011. 3 May 2012. ‹allinthepast.wordpress.com/2011/06/29/cannibalism-and-the-witches-potion/›

"Glossary." Minkisi Figures. Saint Michael's College. 13 Apr. 2012. ‹smcweb.smcvt.edu/amacmillan/African%20Art%20Web/Templates/Glossary.html›

"Kongo Influence in the Americas." African Art Homepage. Saint Michael's College. 13 Apr. 2012. ‹academics.smcvt.edu/africanart/kristen/kongoinfluenceintheamericas.htm›

"mojo." Dictionary.com Unabridged. Random House, Inc. 14 Apr. 2012. ‹dictionary.reference.com/browse/mojo›

"Native American Medicine Bag | Cowboys, Native American, American History, Wild West, American Indians | thewildwest.org." Home | Cowboys, Native American, American History, Wild West, American Indians | thewildwest.org. Cowboys, Native American, American History, Wild West, American Indians | thewildwest.org. 13 Apr. 2012. ‹www.thewildwest.org/nativeamericans/nativeamericansociety/27-nativeamericanmedicinebag.html›

"Sigil - Akashic Records." Akashic Records. 7 May 2012. ‹sanctuary.prelucid.com/library/index.php?title-Sigil#Historical_Uses›

"The Sixth and Seventh Books of Moses." *The Sixth and Seventh Books of Moses.* Ed. Joseph H. Peterson. Twilit Grotto - Esoteric Archives, 2006. 24 Aug. 2012. ‹http://www.esotericarchives.com/moses/67moses.htm›

"The Witch's Formulary and Spellbook by Tarostar." The Witch's Formulary and Spellbook by Tarostar. Abaxion. 01 Apr. 2011. ‹www.abaxion.com/op098.htm›

"Witchcraft Act of 1604 - 1 Jas. I, c. 12." Corvardus' Reliquary. 8 Apr. 2012. ‹www.corvardus.f9.co.uk/religion/wicca/witch1736.htm›

Anastasia. "Africa's Darkest Heart - Broowaha." BrooWaha - Your Citizen Newspaper. BrooWaha, 1 June, 2011. 26 Mar. 2012. ‹www.broowaha.com/articles/9698/africa's-darkest-heart-›

Bathory, Lizza. "O SUBMUNDO: SÃfO CIPRIANO: A MÃ¡gica Do Osso Do Gato Preto (Para Ficar InvisÃvel)." O SUBMUNDO: SÃfO CIPRIANO: A MÃ¡gica Do Osso Do Gato Preto (Para Ficar InvisÃvel). Lizza Bathory. 12 July 2011. ‹lizzabathory.blogspot.com/2010/05/sao-cipriano-magica-do-osso-do-gato.htm›

Bibb, Henry, and Catherine Yronwode. "ON THE USE OF ROOTS AND POWDERS AMONG THE SLAVES." African-American Spirituality: Henry Bibb: Roots and Powders During Slavery Times. Catherine Yronwode. 27 Mar. 2012. ‹www.southern-spirits.com/bibb-roots-powders-slaves.html›

Fortes, Meyers. "FORTES-SOME REFLECTIONS ON ANCESTOR WORSHIP IN AFRICA." CSAC Ethnographics Gallery. Center for Social Anthropology and Computing. 25 Mar. 2012. ‹lucy.ukc.ac.uk/era/ancestors/fortes2.html›

Groover, Mark D., Melanie A. Cabak, and Linda France Stine. "Blue Beads and African American Cultural Symbols." http://mdgroover.iweb.bsu.edu/Stine%20et%20al.%201996.pdf.pdf. Mark Groover. 12 Mar. 2012. ‹mdgroover.iweb.bsu.edu/Stine%20et%20al.%201996.pdf.pdf›

Hoffman, John George. "Pow-Wows Index." Pow-Wows or Long Lost Friend. Sacred Texts. 06 May 2012. ‹www.sacred-texts.com/ame/pow/index.htm› [Other sources make clear the author's name is actually supposed to be John George *Hohman*.]

Karma Zain. "An Instance of Conjure in Georgia." Big Lucky Hoodoo. Karma Zain, 24 Nov. 2007. 27 Mar. 2011. ‹karmazain.livejournal.com/tag /devil%27s%20snuff›

Leland, Charles Godfrey. "CHAPTER IV." Part Two: Chapter IV--EVIL INCANTATIONS. Internet Sacred Text Archive. Sacred Texts. 03 May 2012. ‹www.sacred-texts.com/pag/err/err17.htm›

Leland, Charles Godfrey. "CHAPTER V." Part Two: Chapter V--THE AMETHYST. Internet Sacred Text Archive. Sacred Texts. 03 May 2012. ‹www.sacred-texts.com/pag/err/err18.htm›

Leland, Charles Godfrey. "Part Two: Chapter II--BIRDS AND TREASURES." Internet Sacred Text Archive. Sacred Texts. 6 May 2012. ‹http://www.sacred-texts.com/pag/err/err15.htm›

Leland, Charles Godfrey. "Gypsy Sorcery and Fortune Telling: Chapter V: Charms or Conjurations to Cure or Protect Animals." Internet Sacred Text Archive. Sacred Texts. 6 May 2012. ‹www.sacred-texts.com/pag/gsft/gsft07.htm›

Manning, M. Chris. Buried Bottles: The Archaeology of Witchcraft and Sympathetic Magic. n.p., n.p.. Academia.edu. 14 Apr. 2012. ‹http://ballstate.academia.edu/C hrisManningPratt/Papers/7038 61/Buried_Bottles_Witchcraf t_and_Sympathetic_Magic›

McDavid, Carol. "Kongo Cosmogram." Levi Jordan Plantation. Carol McDavid. 7 May 2012. ‹http://www.webarchaeology.co m/html/kongocos.htm›

Mooney, James. "Sacred Formulas of the Cherokees: Specimen Formulas: To Destroy Life." Internet Sacred Text Archive. Evinity Publishing INC. 16 Apr. 2012. ‹www.sacred-texts.com/nam/cher/sfoc/sfoc53. htm›

Oklahoma Writers' Project. "Martin Luther King - Slavery Interview - Henry F Pyles." Martin Luther King.ca. 1 Mar. 2012. ‹www.martinlutherking.ca/Inte rviews/Henry-F-Pyles.html›

Pepys, Samuel. "Saturday 21 January 1664/65." The Diary of Samuel Pepys. Phil Gyford. 26 Mar. 2012. ‹www.pepysdiary.com/archive/1665/01/21›

Pepys, Samuel. "Friday 20 January 1664/65." The Diary of Samuel Pepys. Phil Gyford. 26 Mar. 2012. ‹www.pepysdiary.com/archive/1665/01/20›

Pepys, Samuel. "Saturday 31 December 1664/65." The Diary of Samuel Pepys. Phil Gyford. 26 Mar. 2012. ‹www.pepysdiary.com/archive/1664/12/31›

Russel, Aaron E. "Material Culture and African-American Spirituality at the Hermitage." http://web.clas.ufl.edu/users/davidson/Kingsley%20Plantation%20Field%20School/Russell%201997.pdf. University of Florida. 12 Mar. 2012. ‹web.clas.ufl.edu/users/davidson/Kingsley%20Plantation%20Field%20School/Russell%201997.pdf›

Viegas, Jennifer. "17th century urine-filled 'witch bottle' found - Technology & science - Science - DiscoveryNews.com - msnbc.com." msnbc.com -

Breaking news, science and tech news, world news, US news, local news- msnbc.com. MSNBC, 4 June 2009. 13 Apr. 2012. ‹www.msnbc.msn.com/id/31107319/#.T4j8he0qNaU›

Wikipedia Users. "Br'er Rabbit." Wikipedia. Wikipedia.org. 1 Apr. 2012. ‹en.wikipedia.org/wiki/Br'er_Rabbit›

Wikipedia Users. "Cannibalism - Wikipedia, the free encyclopedia."Wikipedia, the free encyclopedia. Wikipedia.org. 9 Apr. 2012. ‹en.wikipedia.org/wiki/Cannibalism#African_reports›

Wikipedia Users. "Mummia - Wikipedia, the free encyclopedia." Wikipedia, the free encyclopedia. Wikipedia.org. 12 Apr. 2012. ‹en.wikipedia.org/wiki/Mummia›

Wikipedia Users. "The Great Book of Saint Cyprian - Wikipedia, the free encyclopedia." Wikipedia, the free encyclopedia. Wikipedia.org. 12 July 2011. ‹en.wikipedia.org/wiki/The_Great_Book_of_Saint_Cyprian›

Wikipedia Users. "Clotilde

(slave ship) - Wikipedia, the free encyclopedia." Wikipedia, the free encyclopedia. Wikipedia.org. 29 Mar. 2011. ‹en.wikipedia.org/wiki/Clotilde _(slave_ship)›

Wikipedia Users. "Veneration of the dead - Wikipedia, the free encyclopedia." Wikipedia, the free encyclopedia. Wikipedia.org. 26 Mar. 2012. ‹en.wikipedia.org/wiki/Venerat ion_of_the_dead#Africa›

Windwalker, Barefoot. "The Sacred Bundle." Barefoot's World. Barefoot Bob Hardison. 13 Apr. 2012. ‹www.barefootsworld.net/sacred _bundle.html›

Yronwode, Catherine. "BLACK CAT SPELLS and BLACK CAT SPIRITUAL SUPPLIES." Black Cats. Lucky Mojo Curio Co. 12 July 2011. ‹www.luckymojo.com/blackcat. html›

PRINT

[Various uncredited authors.] *The Devil's Legacy to Earth Mortals.* New York: M. Young: 1884?

"Gris-Gris." *The New and Complete American Encyclopaedia,* Vol. 4: New York: John Low: 1808.

"Popular Names of British Plants." *All The Year Round,* Vol. 10, January 10, 1864. 534 - 539.

"Whisky, Whiskey." The Century Dictionary and Cyclopedia. n.p. New York: The Century Company. 1911.

"Voodoo, or Vaudoux." New *International Encyclopaedia,* Vol. 20. n.p. New York: Dodd, Mead and Co. 1905.

Albertus Parvus Lucius (pseud.) *Secrets Merveilleux de la Magie Naturelle et Cabalistique du Petit Albert.* Lyon: Heritiers de Beringos: 1752.

Albertus Magnus. *Albertus Magnus Being the Approved, Verified, Sympathetic and Natural Egyptian Secrets.* translator n.p. publisher n.p. date n.p. [Probably a 1930s edition.]

Anderson, Jeffrey E. *Conjure in African American Society.* Baton Rouge: Louisiana State University Press: 2005.

Anderson, Jeffrey Elton. "Goofer Dust." *Encyclopedia of African American History.* Santa Barbara, CA: ABC-CLIO: 2010.

Anderson, John Q. "The New Orleans Voodoo Ritual Dance and Its Twentieth Century Survivals." *Southern Folklore Quarterly,* Vol. 24, No. 2. June 1960: 135 - 143.

Anonymous. *The History of the United States for 1796.* Philadelphia: Snowden and McCorkle: 1797.

Anonymous. *Humbug!* New York: Samuel French and Co.: 1859

Anonymous. "Quiz Department." *Meyer Brothers Druggist,* Vol. 28, No. 2. February, 1907. 49.

Anonymous. "Quiz Department." *Meyer Brothers Druggist.* Vol. 28, No. 3. March, 1907: 93.

Anonymous. "Baltimore Bits." *The N.A.R.D. Journal,* Vol. 25, No. 14. 584 - 586. 1918?

Anonymous. "Latest Fads." *Munsey's Magazine,* Vol 16.

October - March 1897, 378 - 380.

Backus, E.M. and Ethel Hatton Leitner. "Negro Tales from Georgia." *Journal of American Folklore,* Vol. 25, No. 96 April-June, 1912. 125 - 136.

Bacon, A. M. "Folk-Lore Scrap-Book" *Journal of American Folklore,* Vol. 9, No. 32, January-March, 1896. 143 - 147, 224 - 226.

Bokie, Simon. "Kongo Religion." *Encyclopedia of African and African-American Religions.* New York: Routledge: 2001.

Bradley, F. W. "The Bo' Dollar." *Southern Folklore Quarterly,* Vol. 25, No. 3, Sept 1961. 198 - 199.

Britten, James, and Robert Holland. *A Dictionary of English Plant-Names.* London: Trübner: 1886.

Buel, James W. *Mysteries and Miseries of America's Great Cities.* St. Louis: Historical Publishing Co., 1883.

Caitlin, George. "The Medicine-Bag and Medicine-

Man of the North American Indians." *The Complete Reader: Book IV. The Senior Class Reader.* London: Longmans, Green and Co., 1868. 215 - 221.

Cavendish, Richard. "Crossroads." *Man, Myth and Magic: An Illustrated Encyclopedia of the Supernatural.* New York: Marshall Cavendish: 1970.

Cristiani, Richard S. *Perfumery and Kindred Arts.* Philadelphia: H. C. Baird: 1877.

Cross, Tom Peete. "Witchcraft in North Carolina." *Studies in Philology,* Vol. 16, No. 3, July 1919. 217 - 289.

Daniels, Cora Linn and C. M. Stephans. *Encyclopaedia of Superstitions, Folklore and the Occult Sciences,* Vol. 3: Milwaukee: J. H. Yewdale and Sons Co.: 1903.

De Laurence, L. W. *The Great Book of Magical Art, Hindu Magic and East Indian Occultism.* Chicago: The De Laurence Company: 1915?

Drake, Samuel Adams. *The Myths and Fables of To-Day.* Boston: Lee and Shepard: 1900.

Evarts, Arrah B. "The Ontogenetic Against the Phylogenetic Elements in the Psychoses of the Colored Race." *The Psychoanalytic Review,* Vol. 3, 1916. 272 - 287.

F. A. S. "Voodooism - Is It a Myth?" *American Anthropologist,* Vol. 1. July 1888. 288 - 289.

Felix, Talia, and Mary Alicia Owen, Lafcadio Hearn, Charles W. Chesnutt, et al. *Voodoo Conjure.* n.p.: Createspace: 2010.

Finck, Henry T. *Primitive Love and Love Stories.* New York: Charles Scribner's Sons: 1899.

Franklin, John. "Franklin's Expedition." *The New Monthly Magazine,* Vol. 7, 1 Jan. 1823: 392 - 400.

Handy, Sara M. "Negro Superstitions" *Lippincott's Magazine* Vol. 48. December 1891, 735 - 739.

Hartland, Edwin Sydney. *Grimm Library: The Legend of*

Perseus. London: David Nutt: 1895.

Haskins, James. *Voodoo and Hoodoo: Their Tradition and Craft as Revealed by Actual Practitioners.* Bronx, NY: Original Publications, 1988.

Hurston, Zora Neale. *Folklore, Memoirs, and Other Writings.* New York: Library of America: 1995.

Hill, Robert Thomas. *Cuba and Porto Rico.* New York: The Century Co.: 1898.

Hyatt, Harry Middleton. *Hoodoo - Conjuration - Witchcraft - Rootwork*: Vol. 1 - 5. Hannibal, MO: Western Publishing Company: 1970 - 1978.

Ingersoll, Ernest. "The Bone in the Black Cat." *Frank Leslie's Popular Monthly*, Vol 28. Jul - Dec 1889. 370 - 371.

Long, Carolyn Morrow. "Grave Decorations." *Encyclopedia of African American History.* Santa Barbara, CA: ABC-CLIO: 2010.

Long, Carolyn Morrow. *Spiritual Merchants: Religion, Magic, and Commerce.*

Knoxville: University of Tennessee: 2001.

Maple, Eric. "Love Magic." *Man, Myth and Magic: An Illustrated Encyclopedia of the Supernatural.* New York: Marshall Cavendish: 1970.

Mathers, S. Liddell Mac Gregor and L.W. de Laurence. *The Greater Key of Solomon.* Chicago: The De Laurence Company: 1914.

Mooney, James. "Folk-Lore of the Carolina Mountains." *Journal of American Folk-Lore,* Vol. 2, No. 5, April-June 1889, 95 - 104.

Moore, Ruby Andrews. "Superstitions in Georgia." *Journal of American Folklore,* Vol. 5, No. 18, July-September, 1892. 230 - 231.

Norris, Thaddeus. "Negro Superstitions." *Lippincott's Magazine,* No. 3, July 1870. 90 - 95

Owen, Mary A. "Among The Voodoos." *International Folk-Lore Congress.* London: David Nutt: 1891. 230 - 248.

Pendleton, Louis. "Notes on Negro Folk-Lore and

Witchcraft in the South." *Journal of American Folk-Lore* Vol. 3, No. 10, Jul - Sept, 1890. 201 - 207.

Puckett, Newbell Niles. *Folk Beliefs of the Southern Negro.* Chapel Hill: University of North Carolina Press: 1926.

Rucker, Walter C. "Grave Dirt." *Encyclopedia of African American History.* Santa Barbara, CA: ABC-CLIO: 2010.

Sisk, Glenn. "Funeral Customs in the Alabama Black Belt, 1870 - 1910." *Southern Folklore Quarterly*, Vol. 22, No. 3, Sept. 1959: 169 - 171.

S. "Voudouism." *The American Practitioner and News*, Vol. 1 & 2: 1886. 56, 57.

Steiner, Roland. "Observations on the Practice of Conjuring in Georgia." *Journal of American Folklore*, Vol. 14, No. 54, Jul - Sept, 1901. 173 - 180.

Thomas, Daniel Lindsey and Lucy Blayney Thomas. *Kentucky Superstitions.* Princeton, NJ: Princeton University Press: 1920.

Unicorn, "Nat Langan's Cat", *Fores's Sporting Notes*, London: Mssrs. Fores: 1902

Wright, A.R., E. Lovett. "Specimens of Modern Mascots and Ancient Amulets of the British Isles." *Folk-Lore*, Vol 29. London: 1908: 288 - 301.

Work, Monroe. "Some Geechee Folk-Lore." *The Southern Workman*, Vol. 35, 1905. 633 - 635

Yronwode, Catherine. *Hoodoo Herb and Root Magic.* Forestville, CA: Lucky Mojo Curio Co.: 2002

Source materials were found by the author online, in her own library, by talking to living practitioners, and by traveling throughout the United States to view special library collections on relevant topics. The author regrets that despite efforts to document all printed sources, a few of them were improperly recorded and therefore could not make it into the bibliography.*

*This is because I am stupid and kept incorrectly writing down the magazine details for the bibliography: there were at least a half-dozen periodical sources where I noted the Author or the Magazine Title but not the issue number or pages, rendering the citation worthless.

28075042R00064

Made in the USA
Middletown, DE
02 January 2016